This book is ~~returned on~~ or before
the last ~~date~~ stamped below.   7/10/13

PILOT

About the Author

ROGER HALL, DFC wrote the original draft of this book soon after the end of the war, when events were still fresh in his memory. He was a long-time supporter of the Battle of Britain Memorial Trust. He died in 2002.

SPITFIRE PILOT

An extraordinary true story of combat in the Battle of Britain

ROGER HALL, DFC

AMBERLEY

Contents

Editor's Foreword

In editing this remarkable narrative by Roger Hall I was set the formidable task of cutting down his original manuscript to just over a third of its length. Nor was it an easy task, for there was so much good material that had to go by the board. Some of the author's descriptions of aerial combat – which are among the most vivid I have ever read – had either to be pruned or completely omitted, but I have retained the full text of those I consider to be quite outstanding. In any event I feel a certain justification in taking this course, since the accounts I have omitted were largely of a technical or repetitive nature, of more interest to wartime pilots than to the general reading public.

However, the main theme of the book lies not so much in the author's experiences as a fighter pilot – which he was for more than two memorable years – as in the fears that beset him throughout the whole of his military career, first in the army and then in the RAF. Many other pilots have written striking accounts of war in the air. Some have sought to glorify aerial warfare and a few, I regret to state, have even indulged in a modicum of self-glorification. Not so Roger Hall. He has had the courage to write the truth about the nagging fears and the mental conflict that obsessed the vast majority of us who flew in the Second World War. On the other hand, he was able to see that there was a peculiar beauty about some aspects of flying and even in the grimness of battle itself.

The reader will find that there is no proper ending to this story. As will become evident, there is no need for one.

J. B.

Introduction

In the summer of 1940 there was a significant threat of a German invasion along the south coast of England. Pilot Officer Roger 'Sammy' Hall was one of the RAF pilots at the forefront of ensuring that the invasion did not take place.

Officially the Battle lasted from 10 July to 31 October 1940 and about 2940 Fighter Command aircrew qualified for the award of the 1939-45 Star with Battle of Britain Clasp for flying operationally in that period. That clasp must be one of the most prized awards in British military history and in the autumn of 2011 there were only around 60 men alive entitled to wear it and to regard themselves as part of Winston Churchill's 'Few'.

The airmen who flew into action then often found themselves having to display great heroism. Some were instinctive killers, but the majority were far from being heroes from the pages of the *Boys' Own Paper*. Before the war many had been farmers, clerks, engineers, school teachers, salesmen and other peace time pillars who had seen reserve organisations, such as the Royal Air Force Volunteer Reserve, as a wonderful means of learning to fly and gaining membership of a flying 'club' without having to pay considerable sums for the privilege.

Many too became reservists because they realised that war was coming and wanted to choose the way in which they took part in it.

When the conflict arrived, most did not have the hatred of the Germans that, for example, their Polish comrades had acquired, but there was a tendency to regard the situation as a frightful cheek when the Hun was flying over England and appeared intent on ending the traditional British way of life.

In his later years I had the honour of knowing Roger Hall and I think it is safe to say that he did not regard himself in any heroic way.

He had set out on a military career in the 1930s, initially becoming a cadet at the Royal Military College, Sandhurst and being commissioned in the Royal Tank Regiment. Mental illness intervened and eventually Roger made a successful application to transfer to the RAF. He trained as a pilot and volunteered for Fighter Command.

On 1 September 1940, as the Battle of Britain was nearing its climax, Roger arrived at the rather sparse airfield at Warmwell, near Dorchester and reported to Squadron Leader Peter Devitt, commanding No 152 squadron. Casualties had been suffered and Roger was one of the replacements.

The squadron had arrived at Warmwell a little under two months previously, with a key purpose of defending the Portland naval base, which was a frequent target for the Luftwaffe.

Flying with his new comrades, Roger experienced the shock of seeing the enemy close at hand, the fear that he spoke of in his title and the insecurities of being thrown into battle with little training or experience.

He did his bit in averting invasion and was eventually awarded the DFC in 1942.

Roger left the RAF in 1944 and, in the post-war world, worked for BEA and, then for 30 years, for the RAC.

When I came to know him in the 1990s he was living in Dover and was a frequent visitor to the National Memorial to The Few, nearby on the cliff top at Capel-le-Ferne.

For the volunteers who ran the site he was a figure to respect, as one of The Few, but also somebody whom they regarded with great affection. This affection manifested itself when 'Sammy' found it increasingly difficult to look after himself. Some of the people from Capel-le-Ferne took it upon themselves to do what they could to help him out.

Roger Hall died in 2002, leaving the legacy of a book, first published a quarter of a century earlier which, until now, has not received the attention it deserves. His greater legacy, of course, was that he was one of the men who ensured the freedom we have today.

Geoff Simpson, 17 October 2011

The National Memorial to The Few

In 1993, Her Majesty Queen Elizabeth the Queen Mother opened the National Battle of Britain Memorial at Capel-le-Ferne. The ceremony was the realisation of a dream for Wing Commander Geoffrey Page, who had been shot down and terribly burned during the Battle, becoming one of the founding members of the Guinea Pig Club. Later in the war Geoffrey would become a wing leader, before crashing and being badly injured again.

The centrepiece of the memorial is a seated airmen in a three-bladed propeller looking out across the English Channel to France. No clues as to his rank are visible, he might be a sergeant or he might be a squadron leader.

Since 1993 the airmen has been joined on the site by the Christopher Foxley-Norris Memorial Wall, on which are listed the Allied airmen who flew in the battle and by full size replicas of Hurricane and Spitfire aircraft from 1940. The Hurricane represents *Little Willie* of No 56 Squadron in which Geoffrey Page was shot down.

Now there are ambitious plans to create a new learning centre at the Memorial. Funds are being raised for this building which will be in the shape of a Spitfire wing and will, indeed, be know as 'The Wing'.

www.battleofbritainmemorial.org

Abbreviations

CO   Commanding Officer
IO   Intelligence Officer
NCO   Non Commissioning Officer
OTU   Operational Training Unit
P/O   Pilot Officer
RFC   Royal Flying Corps
R/T   Radio Telephone
WO   Warrant Officer
WT   Wireless Transmitter

Glossary of Names

Adjutant	F/O Laverack
Peter	Sqn/Ldr P. K. Devitt
Bottle	Flt/Lt D. P. A. Boitel-Gill
Pete	Flt/Lt P. G. St. G. O'Brian, Can.
Cocky	Plt/Off C. S. Cox
Dimmy	Plt/Off L. N. Bayles
Ferdie	Plt/Off F. H. Holmes
Chumley	F/O R. F. Inness
Watty	Plt/Off A. R. Watson
Dudley	Plt/Off W. D. Williams
Sandy	Plt/Off Ballantyne
Fitz	Sgt Fitzsimmons, NZ
Bubbles	Sqn/Ldr Love
Moses	Sqn/Ldr Demozay, (Morlaix), FF
Spud	Flt/Lt R. L. Spurdle, NZ
Bish	F/O Bishop
Heapo	Plt/Off Heap
Jean	Plt/Off J. Marador, FF
Scotty	Plt/Off Downer, NZ
Billy	Plt/Off W. Orr

1
Training: March – August 1940

It was by no capricious whim that, six months after the outbreak of hostilities, during which we had been training in England, I volunteered to transfer to the RAF for the duration of the war.

The romance, the beauty of flight, the ever changing hues of the dawns and the dusks, the serenity of the cloud formation and the vivacity of the sky itself had always enchanted me. It was beautiful. In addition, the thrill of the control of harnessed power ran through my veins like wild horses.

My reading, since childhood, had been predominantly about flying. Immelmann, Boelke, Richthofen and Werner Voss were as familiar to me as were Bishop, Mannock, McCudden and Ball. They were all heroes to me regardless of their race or creed. In the RFC I think there existed a comradeship and respect for friend and foe, born of the dangers suffered and the ecstasy experienced by all who used this new element in which to fight. I was anxious to see if the same spirit had permeated the RAF to which I was so proud to belong.

How I used to thrill to the exploits of the elected few who had climbed so perilously the vertical miles above Northern France – the skies over Arras, the Somme, Bapaume, Mauberge, Ostende and Gravelines – above that vast open plain that was the Pas-de-Calais and the poppy fields of Flanders. The danger of flying seemed little less than that of fighting in those days, and it seemed a miracle that anyone survived at all and a still greater miracle that those who did, remained sane people. Little did I think that I should try to emulate their gallantry twenty-five years later, climbing the same staircase, above the same Pas-de-Calais, and mix it with the sons of those who had shown upon the wingtips of their aircraft the Maltese cross of the Kaiser's Imperial Germanic Air Force. However, it did happen, and each time I flew over that area I was conscious of the fact that it was just here that so many had flown and died and that it was the earth of the Pas-de-Calais which had gathered to itself wrecked aircraft like stub-ends in an ashtray after the grotesque drama that was enacted above. The black Maltese cross had given place to a straight-sided one fringed with white and a swastika embossed upon the tail of the machines in which this new generation of German fighters fought and flew. The RAF retained the red and blue roundel, the same roundel which had gained gradual ascendancy and ultimate mastery over their fathers upon the frail wings of the Camels, the Sopwith pups, the Bristol scouts and the RE8s a quarter of a century before.

I was posted in March 1940 to a small Elementary Flying Training School near Northampton and arrived late in the afternoon in my little two-seater sports car. Before I had been there an hour, I was bundled into a flying kit and parachute and taken up for half an hour by an instructor in a De Haviland Tiger Moth. I had been up once before in my life but this trip was just as novel a sensation as that first, one.

The same evening I met other trainees, ten of them in all, and all similarly transferred army officers. We had one thing at least in common, and that was a desire to prove to ourselves that the air held no terror for us.

After three months' training I became a moderately capable pilot, capable enough anyhow to pass the course. Flying however did not come as naturally to me as I had hoped, and it was more by determination than by prowess that I managed to scrape through. On more than one occasion, because of my ineptitude, carelessness, or downright ignorance, it seemed that my instructor had almost given me up as hopeless. The first of these incidents came soon after my first solo flight. The first time I was allowed to go outside the circuit of the aerodrome for the purpose of practising steep turns I got lost. I searched for the aerodrome for about half an hour and then landed in a field. The episode possibly wouldn't have incurred quite so much disfavour had it not been for the poor testimony for my map-reading ability. However, I scraped through somehow and with the remaining successful ones, lamentably only four, I proceeded up to Scotland in my little car, which was crammed full of luggage.

The machines at this station were very much more the modern counterpart of the service single-seat fighters that were in operation on the Western Front, and comprised all the adjuncts of the Spitfire and Hurricane; retractable wheels, wing flaps, closed-in cockpits, variable-pitch airscrews and, of course, far greater speed.

There lingered on this airfield on the eastern Scottish seaboard tales from the days of the RFC, and among them was the legend of the ghost plane that was to be seen when one of our company was due to die.

Seven from our course died during the first week. We became used to the expectancy of sudden death and all its attendant trimmings. Death was our unwelcome attendant by night and day, and this created in us, whether we knew it or not, some germ of psychosis, the manifestation of which bore different shapes and expressions in each one. It was different from that which one would expect in the trenches, on the high seas or in a submarine. Death was a callous yet prosaic kind of parting – death after breakfast, death before lunch, death in the afternoon, death after the cinema. Death was so casual, yet it was final. One didn't expect to find it among the calm banality of the little Scottish fishing village, among the soft peat-covered moorlands and the windswept coasts.

We all experienced a kind of revolution in living, as indeed it was. There was an outward eccentricity of behaviour, a vulgar acceptance of and indulgence in insobriety; in general a state of mind which the layman could not comprehend.

We developed into what I think of as three-dimensional beings. This term I feel embraces all the little idiosynchrasies of which an airman is made up.

What could others know of the vast and beautiful wastes of interminable rolling cloudbanks above the filth and grime of the city smoke – of the vivid blues and golds among the mountains of the cumulus – of the feathered wisps of cirrus, still, majestic, cold, in the frost-laden upper atmosphere – of the enshrouding white, then grey, then black of the thundercloud and the stark blackness of a moonless night.

It was a world into which we had elected to trespass at whatever cost. It became our world.

It was an exacting education and one which demanded a continuous vigil, the least relaxation of which would tempt misfortune. At one moment we had the arrogance of a god, and at the next the insignificance of a sparrow.

Our three months' training period ran its normal course during which we were initiated into the art and intricacies of formation flying, map-reading, cross-country flying, blind flying, and dogfights. We also learned aerial gunnery, bombing and aerobatics. On the ground we attained adequate proficiency in the theories of flight, and learned how guns fired and what to do if they didn't. We also studied, perhaps not with a great deal of comprehension, or for that matter enthusiasm, the whys and wherefores of service law.

In early August 1940 we left the school, proudly displaying our coveted RAF flying brevets.

We were all eager for operational service and still more for service in a fighter squadron. 'Down south' – as we used to call the battle area – became the ultimate goal of each one of us. The last month had witnessed the imperishable glories and epics of the Battle of Britain. It was therefore only natural for us to want to get involved.

Only three of us realised this all-consuming ambition, not through any superior prowess but solely through the turn of fate.

It was on a summer's evening in August 1940 in the mess of the School of Army Co-operation in Wiltshire that the telephone message summoned us to the chief instructor's office. Only six out of the entire course of twenty-five answered the summons as we were officially off-duty and some had already gone out of the camp. On arrival we were told that three volunteers were required to transfer to fighter squadrons. Naturally we all volunteered and so lots were drawn from a hat by the chief instructor. The atmosphere was tense as the papers were withdrawn from the hat. Mine was the third to emerge.

I arrived the next day at an operational training unit in Cheshire, and reported to the station adjutant who told me that there had been a mistake in my posting and that I was to return to the School of Army Co-operation the next day. My elation dissolved into despair and I walked out of the office as though I had just awoken from a dream. After supper in the mess I went, as was the general custom, into the bar. Before long the adjutant came over and commiserated with me on my bad fortune, remarking that, perhaps, after all, I should live longer as the result of the change of plan. I said, possibly, but in time of war, such motives should not be uppermost in one's mind. He of course agreed and asked me to tell him something of my flying at the station from which I had just come. I started to talk about it and he seemed to register a quizzical sort of expression and I wondered what was worrying him. He stopped me and said: 'You mean to say that you have come from Old Sarum?' I said 'Yes,

I thought you knew that.' He said 'I think there must be some mistake somewhere. We had better go along to the office and sort matters out.' At once I thought that my name had got mixed up with some one else's and for a moment I tried hard to quell my optimism in case it was once again to be dashed to the ground.

It was true! My name had been mixed up with someone else's. I went to my quarters and unpacked.

Fighter Command's losses were so heavy that its intakes were given top priority. I therefore met as my co-trainees, pilots who had transferred from all the other commands in the RAF, including training command.

Next day we were lectured by the station commander. I remember to this day the way he stood there on the platform in the lecture room with his dog, an Alsatian, by his side.

His speech was brief and very much to the point. We were left in no doubt of the exact nature of the demands which the service made on us. We were allowed one week to master the art of aerial fighting in operational service machines with a minimum of twenty-five hours in which to do so. After this we were to be posted to fighter squadrons now fully engaged in the south of England, as combatant pilots. We were to go on leave if we had completed our course before the week was up. Knowing what was required of us, we set to and flew, literally from dawn to dusk. The record for the completed course was two-and-a-half days.

I took four days, packed my bags, flung them into my car and started off to my home to spend what I then considered might well be my last leave with my parents. I hadn't seen Anne for almost a year although we corresponded, but I wished I could have seen her as well.

Ironically enough I was posted to an aerodrome in Dorsetshire only a stone's throw from my old army depot.

I arrived after midnight and the rain was pouring off the roofs of the wooden huts in continuous streams. It was blowing a gale from the sea as it so often did in these parts, and every now and again the downpour became caught up in the wind and driven horizontally. The camp was blacked out; an air raid warning was in progress.

I eventually found the squadron adjutant, who had been expecting me. He told me to pack off to bed and said he would admit me to the honourable membership of 152nd Nizam of Hyderabad's own fighter squadron at 9 o'clock the following morning.

2

Into the Battle of Britain: 1 September 1940

The next day was September the first, 1940. The Battle of Britain was at its full height. Mr Churchill, having visited the French Premier shortly before the collapse of France, stated in the House of Commons that the Battle of France was over and that he expected the Battle of Britain to begin just as soon as Hitler was ready for it. I thought what he had in mind was a land-fought battle on English soil.

Our aerodrome was situated, as the aircraft flies, approximately three miles north-east of Portland Harbour, just behind the hills inland from Weymouth. Our station was in Fighter Command's 10th group and our airfield was an advanced base and satellite of the Wing HQ at Middle-Wallop in Wiltshire. The people were typical of those on a fighter station; both pilots and ground-staff differed in outlook and temperament from those in other commands by the very nature of their duties. Nothing is certain on a fighter station. You never know when you are going to take off. The enemy gives no warning. A fighter station near the coast is more vulnerable to quick air attacks than those inland. The tempo and atmosphere on a fighter station is one of suspense. If the weather were clear one could be pretty certain that, at first light, midday or dusk, action would come sometime and suddenly. It might be in the middle of a game of chess, in the middle of a cup of tea, or just as you were lighting a cigarette, perhaps your last. The telephone, that prosaic little household instrument, would become your absolute master and its monotonous ring would harbinger moments of drama to come. The word 'scramble' became the code for emergency takeoff at the approach of enemy aircraft, which were known as 'bandits', An unidentified aircraft was known as a 'bogey'.

At this time, most unidentified aircraft coming from the south were German and the majority of takeoffs were scrambles.

A squadron consisted of twelve operational aircraft and twelve pilots to fly them. These were naturally augmented by spare aircraft and relief pilots and so a fighter squadron would have possibly half as many aircraft again in reserve to make up the full complement in the event of aircraft being shot down or damaged in combat. Pilots were killed, had to go on leave, and had to have stand down periods, so usually the full complement of pilots in a squadron would be the same number again. Usually half of these would be officers and the remainder warrant officers or sergeant pilots.

The squadron was divided into two flights consisting of six aircraft in each, and a flight was commanded by its flight commander who held the rank of flight lieutenant. Officer pilots apart from the flight commander would either hold the ranks of flying officer or the lowest commissioned rank, pilot officer. The commanding officer of the squadron was a squadron leader. It didn't necessarily follow, however, that the squadron leader always led the squadron and a flight lieutenant a flight. It just depended who was 'on readiness', that is, who was earmarked for duty at the particular time. In the air of course things didn't necessarily work out at all in the way they should do on paper; and after, or even during, a combat the squadron would get split up, flights would get split up, individual sections of two or three machines would get split up, and each pilot and aircraft would become a fighting unit of its own. Ideally of course the squadron should take-off as a squadron of twelve machines and remain as twelve machines throughout the fighting; they should land as twelve machines, too. Sometimes in the mêlée of a fight sections of two or three machines would be able to stay together and sometimes even whole flights, but seldom the entire squadron.

It can be seen then that our own machines might tend to go in opposite directions, as two aircraft travelling in different directions at sometimes three to four hundred miles an hour very soon became separated for good. There were principles to apply but there could, for the reasons stated, be no hard and fast rules to cover every eventuality because, in practice, each of these was different.

There were a number of other factors to contribute to chaos apart from purely enemy tactics and evolutions. They included the unaccountable failures in an aircraft itself. Engine trouble, poor wireless reception, oxygen failure, any of these and other emergencies might necessitate a machine or machines having to leave the formation and thus diminish its effective strength as a fighting unit. The formation leader would then have to improvise and change his formation so as to conserve and make the best use of what remained. The formation leader himself might be, for some reason or other, compelled to leave the formation and the next senior in rank or experience would take over. Everything was flexible – it had to be – and everyone was adaptable for the same reason. A change of situation in the air, from whatever cause, was always met with commonsense and initiative, but commonsense in the air comes only after a considerable amount of experience.

The pilots were necessarily individualist in temperament and usually it was to satisfy this element in their nature that they became fighter pilots in the first place. It was so in my case, and I think others would agree. In the middle of an aerial fight you were really your own master, yet at the same time a member of a team in so far that the safety of the other members was at some times your responsibility though at other times it was not. Very often you were quite on your own and it was then that your individuality was given full reign.

I shall describe only some of the pilots in the squadron for I didn't know them all.

First of all the commanding officer. He was the squadron leader and his Christian name was Peter. He was about twenty-seven at this time, married and with two children. He had been a member of the Auxiliary Air Force before the outbreak of hostilities. Peter was fairly wealthy and had been a member of Lloyd's for some years. He was a debonair sort of a person, an excellent pilot and a very capable leader.

The senior flight commander of 'A' Flight was Flight Lieutenant 'Bottle', or rather that is what he was known as, everyone being known by their nickname or Christian name. Bottle was a tall and slender sort of person and eminently refined in his speech, appearance and behaviour. Everything he did was precise and his skill in the air was second to none. He was thirty-one and before the war he had been a pilot for the old Imperial Airways Corporation.

'B' Flight's commander was a Canadian who went by the name of 'Pete'. He had made the RAF his career and had come over from Canada before the war to attend and graduate from the RAF College at Cranwell. He was therefore probably more acquainted with the service than anyone else in the squadron. He was of medium size with a small dark moustache. He was fairly typical of those who had joined the RAF through Cranwell – thorough and capable.

I was in 'A' Flight and the first person I got to know well was P/O 'Cocky'. He introduced me to the remainder of the flight when I first went down to 'dispersal', the operational centre of the squadron. It was a wooden hut with a telephone and an orderly constantly attending it. This was the telephone that gave us instructions to scramble. There were also twelve beds, ordinary iron beds with mattresses and blankets, arranged on the two sides of the hut. The pilots rested on them when they were at readiness, or even slept on them for the remainder of the night after a pub crawl. To come straight down to dispersal on arrival back from a pub crawl and get into bed was to ensure that one was there for readiness at dawn. If the weather were unsuitable for flying, or, as we knew it, 'unoperational', well then one was able to sleep on undisturbed. Dispersal was so called because outside it the aircraft were dispersed. They were dispersed as an obvious precaution against bombing. They were arranged in a haphazard way to minimise this possibility, although it was as much a token dispersal as anything. They had to be accessible, and it is doubtful if any machine would have escaped a deliberate strafing or even a well placed stick of bombs had an enemy force surprised us.

Of course we weren't there to be surprised, even so the best laid plans of the planners were just as liable to go awry as those of mice and men. Before finishing a description of dispersal, I should say that connected up to each machine was a mobile starter battery. This, as its name implied, was to use its own electrical battery to start the aircraft. The machines were always left facing the inside of the aerodrome so that they could take off immediately in whatever direction they were facing. The pilots usually left their parachutes, during the daytime, on top of the nearside wing of their aircraft with the straps hanging down in front of the leading edge. Thus they were able to dash straight under the wing, clasp the two shoulder straps and pull the body of the parachute off the wing as they moved to the cockpit. They used to leave their helmets, earphones plugged into their sockets, either on the reflector gunsight, which lies just behind the windscreen, or on top of the control column, known generally as the 'stick'. Mechanics – in the RAF jargon 'erks' sat astride the mobile starter boxes attached to all machines in readiness. The erks and their superiors, the NCO and WO mechanics, the chief of whom was known as 'Chiefy', were accommodated at dispersal in tents and marquees. Along with these were all personnel connected with maintenance of the squadron; the petrol bowser crews, the rearmament crews, the wireless servicing crews and the aircraft fitters.

Cocky was a tall fair-haired pilot of about the same age as I was. He had been in the squadron since it was formed at Acklington earlier in the year, and had seen some action on a small scale up in Northumberland before coming south to Warmwell, our present airfield. Cocky was a veteran. He was a very friendly sort of person and sensitive enough to guage the uneasiness of others who felt not quite at home, such as myself. He was a complete extrovert. He would always be ragging like an overgrown schoolboy and he had an apparently inexhaustible supply of energy. He was conscientious and thorough to the point of fanaticism in the air. If there were ever the remotest chance of intercepting a bandit, even in total darkness, Cocky would always have a go.

He introduced me to the others. There was P/O 'Dimmy' who was a red-headed robust sort of person. He had the build you might expect to find in the scrum of a school first fifteen. He gave you the impression of brute force without much refinement, but he was by no means a crude pilot. On the contrary, he had excelled himself since the squadron had come down south. He was married, and people thought that this had in some way imposed a newly acquired caution upon him, a caution which, before his marriage, had not existed. He seemed to be trying to resist an inner conflict, one side of which was trying to restrain him and the other, the more natural side, to live and fight as though he had no wish to live for ever.

F/O 'Ferdie', usually known as 'the Bull' since his first name was Ferdinand, was small, unassuming and balding. He was past thirty and had been an instructor in the early days of the war; for this reason his flying was exact, and if at times he gave the impression that he was being foolhardy, it was only one's own ignorance and inexperience which made one think so. The Bull was an expert in all forms of bad-weather flying and if one were fortunate enough to be flying with him in bad weather there was never any reason to feel apprehensive. Ferdie always got back to base somehow. In action he was cool and calculating but not a fire-eater, and I think his comparative caution was due not to any lack of aggressiveness, but to a studious and analytical turn of mind.

F/O Inness, better known as 'Lord Chumley', was another with whom I was to become more intimately acquainted before long. He was perhaps the most amusing of all the characters in the squadron. He was an old Etonian and his behaviour, manner and speech all betrayed the fact unmistakably! This was not to say that he was in any way a pompous or patronising person or that he regarded others of less exalted upbringing with disfavour or as in any way inferior. On the contrary, as a product of that great school, he comprised all the virtues including tolerance towards others which characterised the majority of those who went there. He was typical of OEs in the respect that he could obviously have been at no other school and without wishing to get into any deeper water I'll leave it at that.

Finally, there was P/O 'Watty'. He was very young, not yet twenty years old. He came to the squadron shortly before I did, and he and I became friends almost at once. He had arrived at the station about a week before and was very proud of the fact that he had already been in action more than once.

The first time I met him he was casting envious glances at my car, which, being almost new, did create more than the usual amount of curiosity. He approached me and in a somewhat callous manner, I thought at the time, asked me if he could have it if I were killed before he was. I said 'Of course, you can,' thinking at the same time how very realistic these people were in their attitude to life and death and yet how natural had seemed the ingenuousness of such a remark. Watty I think was one of those people who by their very refusal to be taught, was fated to die young, especially in such a game as this. He was far too overconfident in his approach to the whole business and he had the added disadvantage of having shot a Junkers 88 down on his first operational sortie. I say a disadvantage because this event served, from his point of view, to assure him that he knew all the answers. If the converse of this state of mind were in any way a reliable guide to one's life expectancy, then I felt sure that I should die an old man.

Before lunch I went to report to the squadron adjutant. The 'Adj' as he was affectionately known to all and sundry was a middle-aged man who had seen service as a soldier in the previous war. He was one of the many who, having been a regular soldier, was axed when he was too young to retire, and found sanctuary and companionship in the administrative branch of the RAF.

The general discipline and administration of the squadron on the ground was invested in the Adj and although he gave one the general impression that he never did any work, this was merely because he took such pains to prevent the pilots from being worried by petty restrictions and red tape which could serve no useful purpose. The Adj seemed to form a sort of absorbent buffer upon whom all the troubles of the squadron fell, were sorted out, and resolved one way or another without any fuss. We seldom gave him credit for the job he did.

When I entered his office, he spoke to me as father to son and made certain I had everything I needed. He then took me in to see the CO whose office was next door to his. The CO told me to go down to dispersal and report to my flight commander. I was to be in 'A' Flight and therefore my flight commander would be Bottle.

It was a good mile from the station offices to the dispersal hut so I got into my car and drove down there. I identified myself to Bottle and was told to get kitted up with parachute and 'Mae West' from the stores and report back after lunch. I got back into the car and eventually found the parachute store which was tucked away in a remote part of the camp. The corporal in charge of the store fitted me out and made one or two adjustments to the straps before I collected the 'Mae West' and microphone from the W/T store. I pushed these with the parachute into the back of the car and went up to the mess for lunch.

In the ante-room I met the Adj again and he asked me what I was going to have. We had a pint each and I asked him to tell me about the squadron and what they had done since they had been down there. He must have gauged a certain anxiety in my voice, for he discounted most of my fears and reassured me on others before going on to topics of his own. I felt better, and I soon realised that it was this waiting that was unnerving me more than anything else. I must get into the air this afternoon, I felt. The end door of the ante-room burst open and some of the pilots came in on their way to lunch. They were in uniform but with high-necked jerseys of various colours and flying boots. Some had thick oiled wool stockings turned down over the top of their boots. The Adj called them all by their first names or nicknames and they all called him 'Adj' in return.

After lunch I went down to dispersal again ready for flying. 'B' Flight were at readiness now and 'A' Flight were getting ready to go up to the mess for lunch. It was always like this. Only one flight was allowed up to the mess at the same time unless weather conditions made flying impossible when perhaps the entire squadron might be in the mess at the same time.

Before he went, Bottle told me to wait till he got back and said he would then take me up in formation to see how I shaped. I was glad that I was going to fly again at last and only hoped that my flying would satisfy him. I sat around rather self-consciously while 'B' Flight settled themselves down on the beds, fully kitted up. Some were smoking, some reading and some even trying to snatch some sleep. A few of the more boisterous ones were doing their best to prevent this by ragging about and generally behaving rather like one used to do at school before the lights went out in the dormitory.

The telephone rang and the orderly, phone in one hand and pencil in the other, kept on saying 'Yes –, Yes,' as he jotted something down on the pad in front of him. People stopped ragging and all faces turned towards the orderly with the telephone. With a final 'Yes, Sir,' he replaced the receiver and said 'Blue Section to patrol Portland – angels twenty.' This wasn't a scramble, it was merely a precautionary patrol ordered by Group HQ, possibly because they had got some sort of idea that a raid might develop in that area. No one knew, but Blue Section took their time getting off the ground, walking almost casually over to their aircraft. 'B' Flight's commander was leading Blue Section and with him was one of the sergeants and P/O 'Greeno', as he was known to his flight.

The three aircraft started up and, with Pete leading, taxied out slowly to the takeoff position. When they were in their positions, one on either side of the leader, Pete waved his hand fore and aft to indicate that he was ready to start rolling, and this was acknowledged by the other two with a thumbs up signal.

The three aircraft moved off, apparently as one machine. The noises of the individual engines gradually became absorbed by one another until the sound from them was that of one vast throbbing and pulsating bit of machinery. They left the ground about half way down the grass airfield and, rocking slightly as they pumped their undercarriages up, continued to fly straight on, climbing slowly. Each machine left a long line of blackish vapour behind it which gradually dispersed as they got further away. Then they turned gently to port, now climbing more steeply, and headed out to sea. I watched them until they disappeared towards the sun and wondered what lay in store for them.

Some time later 'A' Flight returned from the mess and Bottle went over and had a word with Chiefy to see if there were an aircraft to spare that I could use. He came back with a rather despondent expression on his face to say that there wasn't one and I would have to wait until after tea. I decided to go back to my quarters and finish my unpacking, feeling rather redundant.

I got into my car again and just as I had turned into the road from the mud lane leading to dispersal I heard a lot of excited voices and a general commotion coming from the hut. Almost at once an engine burst into life, then another and another until nine machines had been started up. I realised that this was a scramble. The nine planes which, with Blue Section, made up the whole squadron were about to take off. Pilots were running fast towards their machines and one or two were already taxi-ing out to their takeoff positions as I stopped my car to watch.

One by one the nine machines formed up into a fairly shallow sort of 'V' formation on the ground and with a signal from the leader, Bottle I presumed, there was a gradually deepening note from the engines and the whole body of aircraft started to move forward. They moved slowly at first, until after a hundred yards or so the tail of each individual machine rose from the ground. Then they gathered speed perceptibly and shortly afterwards they left the ground. It was an impressive sight. I wondered how long they would be up and if I should get my flight in after tea. I wondered where the squadron was going to, what they would meet and whether they would all come back safely, I wondered a lot of things and as I got back into the car I offered a silent prayer.

From the ante-room I heard some machines return about an hour and a half later. I decided to stay in the ante-room feeling that if they wanted me down at dispersal they would surely call for me. I knew they would be fully occupied with other and more important things.

There was no call for me that evening. The squadron had returned, that is ten of them. They had joined up with Blue Section over Southampton, apparently, whither Blue Section had been redirected and had come into a large formation of Dornier 17 bombers with an escort of ME 109 single engined fighters. From what I could gather from the conversation in the mess afterwards, they had accounted for four of the bombers when they were attacked by the escort from cloud cover. One pilot from 'A' Flight was shot down in flames by one of these. Almost simultaneously, another, a sergeant pilot from 'B' Flight, went down out of control, plunging straight into the Solent.

3

On Readiness: Dawn, 2 September 1940

Bottle told me not to bother about my formation flight with him, but to be on readiness in Red Section at dawn the following day. To be at readiness at dawn, one had to be at dispersal by five o'clock. I decided in view of this to have an early night. I didn't feel myself to be quite part of the squadron yet and so I didn't feel inclined to have a beery night in the mess. I went off to my quarters shortly after nine having left a request for an early call with the mess waiter before leaving.

I prayed a lot before trying to go off to sleep. I prayed hard and earnestly for the courage that I knew I should require, and of which I felt in such dire need.

I slept quite a bit that night although I was awake well before I was called at four-thirty by my batman with a cup of tea. I gulped it down, got up and shaved. I was the first to get to the mess and was quickly served with a good helping of porridge by the WAAF waitress on duty. Dimmy was the next to come in, with his tunic coat still undone, and combing his hair as he sat down. 'Operational already?' he queried, looking at me. I said 'Yes.' 'Good show,' he replied. The other two, Ferdie and Cocky, came in shortly afterwards and both of them made some sort of sign of recognition before starting their meal. Nothing much was said that was of any consequence during breakfast except possibly an occasional reference to the weather. The weather was always of consequence, for when it was good we flew and when it wasn't we sometimes didn't, but the reason we didn't or weren't likely to, was because the Germans didn't either.

As I arrived outside the hut, at dispersal, the merest glimmer of the impending dawn showed itself over to the east. It was too early yet to judge what sort of day it would herald but we could reasonably expect another cloudless day. A kind of Indian summer had persisted for the preceding two or three weeks and, although it was officially autumn now, the heat of the previous days hardly gave that impression. 'M' for mother was dispersed a long way from the hut and after some difficulty I found it. The machine was soaked with dew and I laid my parachute on a tarpaulin lying by the tail wheel, before clambering on to the port wing to open up the cockpit hood. The inside of the hood was wet with condensation but otherwise the cockpit itself seemed to be fairly dry and I got inside. I released the adjustable seat down to its furthest ratchet and turned the revolving foot screws on each rudder control column until the rudder bar itself was at its fullest extent. Then I got out of the machine to retrieve my parachute. I placed this in the seat recess and sat on it, at the same time doing up the harness straps. I then plugged my wireless receiving lead, attached to the earphones of my helmet, into its socket on the right side of my seat. I put my helmet on and fastened up my cockpit straps which are known as the 'Sutton harness'. These are common to all aircraft and are presumably named after the man who invented them. They are designed to hold the pilot securely in the cockpit and yet are fastened in such a way that he can undo them within seconds.

Having assured myself that the harness was properly adjusted, I began to check over the machine itself. Before flying, it is always necessary to carry out a cockpit drill. The main essentials of it are to ensure that, in the first place, the petrol cocks are securely turned on, and the throttle control lever has sufficient friction to ensure that it stays where it is placed when one's hand is removed from it, as from time to time it has to be. Apart from this it is essential to see that the fine adjustment to the elevator and aileron trim is in its correct setting. If this is not right, the effect, sometimes disastrous, will become apparent only when the aircraft is beginning to gain its flying speed. If it is trimmed too far forward or in a nose-down position, it will be difficult to get the aircraft off the ground, and if in a nose up position, it will tend to get off the ground before it has enough flying speed and will probably stall. If the rudder or the aileron control surfaces are incorrectly trimmed, a formation take-off will become dangerous, for these remote controls will begin to show their effect as soon as the tail of the aircraft is lifted from the ground and if extremely trimmed one way or the other, the effect would be to throw the aircraft to one side. It can be seen that cockpit drill is essential, not just once a week or once a day but before every single take-off. The petrol supply in the tank and the oxygen container had also to be checked. The wireless had to be checked for reception and the luminous gun-reflector-sight for its clarity.

Having checked everything and left my parachute inside the cockpit, I slid the hood forward to keep it dry and made my way back to the hut. Inside the others were wrapped up in blankets and trying to sleep. I settled myself on one of the beds nearest the door and lit a cigarette trying to gain some sort of composure.

It was shortly before 7 o'clock when the telephone rang. The orderly lifted the receiver and almost at once shouted 'Red Section scramble. Base angels ten.' I was up like a shot and out of the door before the others. I had a comparatively long way to go to my machine and I ran hard all the way. My mechanic was already at the starter battery when I got there. I leant on to the trailing edge of the port wing and slid open the cockpit hood, opened the small door underneath and got in. My mechanic was on the wing now and helping me to get into my parachute harness. I fumbled with it, my fingers shaking all the time. The parachute was fixed and the mechanic was holding the two upper straps of the Sutton harness above my shoulders waiting for me to fix the right lower one. Eventually all was set and I grabbed my helmet and put it on. My mechanic had taken up position again at the starter battery and was anxiously awaiting my signal to press the button. I switched the petrol and two magneto switches on and gave the priming pump three injections. I put my thumb up and received acknowledgement from the mechanic who then pressed his button. At the same time I pressed both mine and the propeller started to turn. It fired after a few turns and blue exhaust swept past the open cockpit. The mechanic leant forward and uncoupled the lead from the starter battery, pulling the wheel chocks away at the same time. Finally he gave me the all clear signal and I opened the throttle to taxi towards the takeoff point, at the same time making a cursory last minute cockpit check as I went.

Cocky and the sergeant pilot who, with me, made up Red Section, were just getting into position as I got there. I turned my machine to the left, using full left rudder and at the same time applying hand brake pressure from the lever on the stick. The machine slewed round nicely and I took up my position on the left side of Cocky. After a thumbs up signal to him to let him know that all was in order, Cocky opened his throttle and we started to move. Keeping an unrelaxing gaze towards his machine the three of us gathered speed rapidly. I saw Cocky's wheels leave the ground and at once felt my own free themselves. I eased out a bit to the left as Cocky flying as Red one, retracted his undercarriage and in doing so rocked his machine about a bit. This was almost inevitable for you had to change hands, the left hand from the throttle to the stick and the right hand from the stick to the wheel retracting lever. The small lock lever had to be moved fore and aft with a pumping action until the wheels finally locked themselves with a click into the wing recesses. The red light then appeared on the dashboard which meant 'wheels up'. This operation, although tedious to describe, took really very little time in practice but it always involved rather a lot of rocking about in the air.

By the time we had finally taken off not much more than three minutes had elapsed since the telephone had rung in the hut.

I was Red three and the sergeant pilot was Red two in the formation. Red one led us into a fairly steep spiral climb over the airfield, turning to the left. I was on the inside of the turn and therefore my speed was the slowest, not being much more than 160 mph. We were climbing at a rate of about two thousand feet a minute with quite a lot of throttle. There was an indistinct crackle coming into my earphones but nothing coherent. Shortly before we got to ten thousand feet I started to turn on my oxygen supply. When we had reached this altitude we levelled off and I heard 'Hallo Mandrake – Hallo Mandrake – Maida Red one calling – are you receiving me?' At once in reply came 'Hallo Red one – Red one – receiving you loud and clear – what are your angels?' – 'Hallo Mandrake – Maida Red one answering – angels ten – over.' 'Hallo Red one, there is one bandit over Chalkpit same angels, Victor 130 degrees – buster.'

'Hallo Mandrake, your message received and understood, listening, out.' Looking at my code card for the day I identified 'Chalkpit' as being Southampton and we seemed to be almost halfway there. The code word 'buster' urged one to hurry.

'Hallo Red Section – Red one calling – Line astern – line astern'. I moved out to the left while Red two slid in behind and underneath Red one, and then I came behind and underneath Red two.

In order to avoid being upset by a machine's slipstream when flying in line astern it is necessary to keep below the machine in front. The view one got from this position was of the underside of your leader's fuselage and tail through the upper part of your windscreen and the fore part of your hood.

We were now travelling at about three hundred miles an hour with almost full throttle, but without having sighted the bandit.

It was quite light now, and to the south-east the sky was clear. The sun, recently risen, was not far above the land to our port front. Below, the ground was darker and there were patches of whitish mist lying in some of the valleys. Occasionally there was the reflection of the sun from a window or from the top of a greenhouse or something. The air was calm and there were hardly any bumps. Everything seemed to be going smoothly and I had become more composed. I wondered how I would feel when, and if, we were to find the bandit.

I didn't have to wait long, for over the radio came 'Hallo Mandrake, hallo Mandrake – Maida Red one calling – Tally ho – Tally ho.' This latter was the code employed for announcing that a bandit was sighted.

Almost at once came the reply 'Hallo Maida Red one, Hallo Maida Red one – Mandrake answering – good show and the best of luck – Mandrake listening – out.' This acknowledgement was merely a background to my thinking, for Red one's tally ho had imposed a completely new sensation on me, one which I had never before experienced. I find it difficult to describe. At one and the same time I felt both fear and elation, the one attempting to crush me, the other trying to raise me to inexpressible heights. I looked about me for the bandit which Cocky had spotted, but could see nothing. 'Loosen up the formation Red Section – break right after attack' came through my earphones. I adjusted my reflector gun sight and turned the safety catch of my gun button to 'Fire'. We had loosened up the formation quite considerably now and there was a distance of about twenty yards or more between the machines to allow plenty of freedom of action and manoeuvre.

Now I saw it! It was a little below us off our starboard quarter. It seemed somehow quite incongruous here above the English countryside. It was black and unfamiliar, unfamiliar to me for I had never seen a German aircraft before. It was a Junkers 88 twin-engined bomber. It looked identical to the silhouettes of it on posters and in aircraft recognition books. It had straight-sided black crosses on the ends of each wing and these were immediately conspicuous because they were bordered with white lines. It was twisting and turning as we were coming down to attack it. It had seen us, there was no doubt of that, for from behind each of its engine nacelles issued a long black stream of oily vapour betraying the fact that it was travelling at full throttle. We ourselves were travelling at little less than three hundred and eighty mph and were coming in behind it after a shallow diving turn to starboard.

In front of me Cocky and Red two, some distance behind him, were holding their machines fairly steady and I, some way behind Red two, kept my machine in much the same state. I was impatient to see Cocky open fire but still nothing happened. I was seized with a sadistic sort of curiosity to see what the result of our fire was going to be. I had never seen an aircraft crash or explode or break up in the air and the prospect of it now somehow filled me with a curiosity which, if it did nothing else, served in some measure to dispel my own fear of being shot down by the German rear gunner.

The Junkers 88 was keeping a steady course now, presumably to give its rear-gunner a chance. The chance seemed to have gone though, for as Cocky broke off his attack and pulled his machine sharply up to the right the port engine of the Junkers 88 was alight. Flames were coming from it and, behind these, long streams of thick black smoke poured. Red two was now attacking the machine's starboard engine, or so I presumed; it seemed the obvious thing to do, but then, in the air, at times nothing seems very obvious nor are events always what you might expect.

The Junkers 88 exploded, Red two may have been attacking the starboard engine for all I know, but I didn't know and nobody did or ever would, for the exploding aircraft engulfed Red two, absorbed it, became integrated with it, and the intermingled mass of flaming wreckage fell into the sea and nothing was recovered. I was able to pull away to port as a few fragments from the bomber hit the under surface of my main plane without inflicting any damage. I had not fired a shot myself and I felt a revulsion as I pulled my machine hard up to starboard to rejoin Cocky.

Momentarily I felt all fear disperse and give place to a sort of maniacal hatred which was unnatural. It was the hatred of an ungovernable anger. I can't adequately describe it but I felt certain that if I were called upon to engage the enemy again while this feeling persisted, I should find it difficult to control myself and I should have no heed for my own safety and give no quarter to anyone.

'Hallo Mandrake – Hallo Mandrake' Cocky called up. 'Maida Red one calling. Bandit destroyed – Red two lost also – over.' That's all he said. 'Hallo Maida Red one – Hallo Maida Red one – Mandrake answering, your message received – understand bandit destroyed – Good show – Pancake – Pancake – Mandrake to Maida Red one, over.'

As we flew back I came up in Vick formation with Cocky and felt some sort of reassurance by watching him inside his cockpit. 'Pancake' was the code word for return to base and land. I was glad we were going back for I badly felt the need to talk to someone on the ground; for anything to happen to expunge the sight of what I had just seen. In a way I was, I think, glad that this sort of thing had happened to me quickly for I now no longer harboured any illusions about this business. I had read about it in the papers, I had heard about it on the news and from others, most of whom had had little experience of it at first hand and now I knew at last what really did happen. The gulf that existed between what one was led to believe from these sources and what in fact happened, was too wide to contemplate. On the way home as we dived down to the lower stratus I thought of Red two as he had been but three-quarters of an hour before; asleep, wrapped up in a blanket at dispersal. I don't think I had even seen his face and I hardly knew his name. I thought of where he was now, in the sea, not far off from where he had spent his last night, at Bournemouth. I tried not to think of it at all. I felt that I should be quite useless as a fighter pilot if I couldn't control my thoughts and imagination. I should have to become callous and cold and ruthless. I thought of what all the others had seen already and of how they too must, at one time, have been thinking what I was thinking now but had mastered their thoughts. They must have done, otherwise they would not have still been with the squadron, but they were. Sooner or later I should have to become callous and I consoled myself with the thought that it was really better that it should be sooner.

We came in sight of the aerodrome, now bathed in pale sunlight and Cocky started to throttle back his engine, at the same time easing his stick back to keep the nose of his aircraft up and thereby lose his speed more quickly. The wheels of a Spitfire must not be let down when the aircraft is travelling at more than 180 mph and so the first thing to do for landing procedure is to lose speed to this extent.

When this has been accomplished the small selector lever on top of the wheel retracting gear is placed in the free position and the wheels become disengaged from their locknuts and swing free from their wing recesses under their own weight. They have to be pumped down however by the same procedure as before with the aid of the large pump handle until they are securely locked down. The green light then replaces that of the red on the dashboard, illuminating the letters 'Wheels down'. This of course is accomplished in a very short space of time in practice and is second nature to a pilot. Before landing the airscrew pitch control lever is placed in the fully fine position so that, in the event of having to go round again after a bad landing, the airscrew will already be in the fine position. All take-offs must be made like this. Finally the wing flaps must be lowered. These act as air brakes, thus slowing the machine down while still airborne, and also provide the aircraft with more lift, thereby giving it a much slower landing speed. The wing flaps on a Spitfire must never be lowered at speeds above 140 mph.

Cocky signalled to me to say that he was about to lower his wheels. This was a custom that was entirely necessary, for when aircraft are in close formation, as those in any fighter squadron usually were except perhaps in battle, the individual machines are tucked, the one beside or behind the other at distances which are sometimes measured only by inches.

When I saw Cocky's wheels come down I lowered my own and opened my sliding hood. This again is part of the drill, the idea being that if for any reason the aircraft turns over on its back on landing the pilot should be able to get out. The fresh air as it poured into my cockpit was revitalising and I felt glad of it. As we approached the last leg of our circuit, still about five hundred feet from the ground, Cocky gave me the flaps-down signal and I depressed my own lever. 'Hallo Mandrake – Maida Red one about to pancake,' was our last message to control. We touched the surface of the aerodrome about half way down its length and with the application of a little brake-pressure pulled up about three hundred yards further down. 'Hallo Red three, Red one calling – break off and taxi in independently' was Cocky's last instruction to me. I taxied my aircraft back to its former dispersal point, turned it round to face the inside of the aerodrome and pulled the engine cut-out lever. The propeller stopped turning and I switched the magneto switches off, turned the petrol cocks off, and the oxygen turncock behind the armour-plated seat and the radio switch. I removed my helmet and placed it on the reflector-sight, opened the small cockpit door on my left side and stepped out on to the edge of the wing root near the cockpit. I removed my parachute and placed it on the leading edge of the port wing with the top straps hanging down over it. My mechanic was there to help me and asked me whether I had had any luck. The mechanics always displayed an intense interest in the activities of the pilots, especially those who were flying the machines which they themselves were servicing. I gave him a brief account of what had happened and that was all I could say or felt like saying. My mechanic appeared to register the same incredulity that I myself was feeling. I looked at my watch and it was not yet eight o'clock. All this had happened, incredibly, within the last three-quarters of an hour.

I walked back to the hut while the petrol bowser was refuelling Cocky's machine and the armament crews were reloading his guns. I met Cocky at the door of the hut and he gave me an outsized grin of reassurance, as he saw my worried countenance. I felt very small and humble. 'Well, that was a bit of a shambles wasn't it? Bloody 88. The bastard.' That was the only reference he made to the episode. I supposed this was the only attitude to adopt. 'Brains', our intelligence officer, was the first to greet us at the door of the hut, pencil and notebook in hand. This was his prerogative, moreover his job, to get the first account of a combat. He wanted to know its exact nature, how many machines there were, what was the location with relation to the ground, at what height the enemy was first seen, at what distance it was first attacked, by whom, and what was the general duration of each burst of fire and of the whole attack, and what was the result of the attack. In fact Brains wanted to know everything from A to Z, and in detail. He would then sift his report and after collating it, telephone the whole of it to Group Intelligence. What they did with it was anybody's business but they wanted it all and they certainly got it all.

In point of fact the machine which had been destroyed was a reconnaissance aircraft sent to report on cloud and weather conditions and to take photographs of the previous night's raid on Southampton. A reconnaissance aircraft at this time of day usually fore-ran a massed raid later on in the day. We wondered whether they would send another. Green Section were the next section to scramble and went off, Ferdie leading, about a quarter of an hour after we had landed. They were scrambled to angels twenty over

Portland. At half-past eight 'B' Flight came to relieve those of us who had been on dawn readiness, to enable us to get up to the mess for a short while and make good the shortcomings that our early call had inevitably inflicted upon us. We were able to have a reasonable shave and a second breakfast if we wanted it. As soon as 'B' Flight had taken over from us we got back into the 15 cwt. truck and were driven up to the mess. On the way we stopped at the sergeant's mess to deposit the remaining sergeant pilot who had been on readiness with us.

I was glad of this respite, short though it was, for it tended to freshen one up a bit and this, in turn, always had a beneficial effect on one's outlook and that all important yet intangible thing, one's morale. There was no doubt about it, morale was a very real thing and the state of one's personal morale depended almost entirely upon the small, but apparently inconsequential things, such as the sort of breakfast you had had, whether the tea was hot or cold, whether you had managed to get a good shave from your old razor blade, whether your batman had cleaned your buttons well, whether your cigarette case was full when you left the mess for dispersal and a hundred and one other little things.

'A' Flight returned to dispersal at half-past nine, We were, by agreement between the flight commanders, allowed an hour up at the mess before coming back to readiness. But like so many other things at this time, nothing was certain, nothing could be taken for granted and the length of our respite depended entirely upon the telephone. If Group HQ thought fit to recall us, then back we went to dispersal, whether we were in the middle of a shave or halfway through breakfast or not. We seldom had the hour that we considered was our due.

At half-past nine the squadron as a whole was at readiness and this fact was made known to 'Group' by the orderly at the telephone. Not infrequently the Controllers at Group were ex-members of the squadron, having a spell on the ground as a rest from the intense fighting of the previous two months. Therefore they kept a special interest in the activities of the squadron, some of the pilots they had known and spoke to them on the telephone with the minimum of formality – or decorum. The pilots were able to find out from them what was 'On the board'. This expression was used universally throughout Fighter Command and it meant that the plots of enemy aircraft received by radar, having gone through the filter-room at Fighter Command HQ at Stanmore were placed on our Group HQ operation board. We were able from this information to get some sort of an idea of whether we were likely to receive a scramble, and if so when, and how many of us they would want. The Controllers were always helpful and obliging, knowing our difficulties our feelings and our petty trials.

At ten to eleven the telephone rang and the orderly, having answered it, laid the receiver on the table and got up from his chair. He came over to the bed on which Bottle was lying and said: 'Excuse me, Sir but the Controller would like a word with you.' Bottle got up, cigarette and holder in hand as always, and came over to the table. He picked the telephone up and a conversation ensued. What's the form, Bottle?' said Dudley, another 'A' Flight pilot, when he had finished. Bottle getting back to his bed and picking up his book again, quite imperturbable, said: 'Group might need us in the next half hour; apparently they have a hundred-plus on the board over the Cherbourg peninsula – they're not coming our way yet though. To be on our toes sort of nonsense, Tommy's controlling'. 'It's fine enough for a Blitz, I suppose,' said Dudley. 'A' Flight comprised Red, Yellow and White Sections while 'B' comprised Blue, Green and Black. In the event of a squadron scramble 'A' Flight always led with 'B' Flight in whatever position the commander of 'A' Flight wanted them to be. Sometimes the squadron would take-off together as twelve machines or separately in two Flights, the one following the other. It depended on events and circumstances, but to the greatest extent, I think, on common sense.

The ideal take-off was always made in 'V' formation, whether it was by Flights or by the entire squadron. In the case of 'A' Flight, Red one would form the spearhead of the 'V' with Red two on his immediate left. To the left of Red two would be Yellow one and to his left, Yellow two. On Red one's immediate right, White one would take up his position and, to his right, White two. Once airborne, Red two would fall in behind Red one, Yellow two behind yellow one and white two behind white one. Similarly, 'B' Flight would arrange its Blue, Green and Black Sections. Thus in the air the Flight would form itself into two ranks of three machines in 'V' formation or, in the case of the entire squadron, two ranks of six machines in the same formation. Ultimately, the smallest unit would be a single section and if possible these should always stick together whatever happened, but even this was impossible at times.

Normally, one Flight was allowed to go to lunch up at the mess at half-past twelve while the other remained on readiness. But today, at twenty-past, the telephone rang and the orderly answering it, said: 'Squadron scramble Southampton angels twenty-five.'

4

First Combat: September 1940

I was flying White two behind Ferdie as White one. The new Yellow Section in 'A' Flight was made up from a F/O just returned from leave and a new sergeant pilot who had arrived at the station from OTU (Operational Training Unit) that very day. Black two was now P/O Watty, who had been standing down during the morning.

In the absence of the CO, Bottle was leading the squadron as Red one and Maida leader. We taxied out and formed up in squadron formation for take-off. Bottle always seemed to prefer it this way when he was leading. White Section were on the port outside of the 'V' and with a fore and aft movement of his hand Bottle started to move, the remainder of the squadron opening up their engines simultaneously.

It must have looked an impressive sight, I thought, to anyone watching from the ground. The noise must have seemed deafening as the twelve 'Merlin' engines reached their ultimate boost for takeoff.

Off the ground, we quickly slid into position, the number two's behind their number ones and the whole of 'B' Flight slightly behind 'A' Flight. Turning to port gently Bottle called up control to say that Maida squadron were now airborne. Control answering confirmed that we were to patrol base at angels ten. We continued to spiral round the aerodrome gaining altitude at the rate of approximately two thousand feet a minute. At ten thousand feet we levelled out and Bottle called up to say that we were now in position. Control acknowledged his call and said that for the present we were to stay put.

For about ten minutes we remained over the airfield, which, as we looked down on it, seemed a compact little affair difficult to reconcile with what from the ground appeared to be nothing more than a number of wooden huts of various sizes strung together in a haphazard fashion. I could see it now as the planners must have seen it on the drawing board. Looking to the east I could see a few miles away my old regimental depot with its tank-tracks leading conspicuously away from the buildings over the heather to the driving and testing grounds.

'Hallo Maida leader' called up control, 'Increase angels to two-five – increase your angels to two-five – Mandrake to Maida leader – over.' 'Hallo Mandrake, Maida leader answering – understand angels two-five – listening and out,' came the reply from Bottle.

Once again we started to climb, this time very steeply in an attitude which was generally known as 'hanging on the prop'. My airspeed was not much in advance of 140 mph which was not at all comfortable as it precluded any sudden change of direction should it have become necessary. The aircraft was not far from its stalling speed.

'Hallo Maida leader, Mandrake calling – Hallo Maida leader – Victor 080 degrees – angels three-zero – over.'

'Hallo Mandrake – Maida leader answering – your message received and understood – Vectoring 080 degrees, angels three-zero – listening out.'

We had reached thirteen thousand feet when this order came through and, still climbing, we started on our new course which was a little north of due east and would bring us into the region of South London.

'Hallo Maida leader – Mandrake calling – What are your angels?' called control. 'Hallo Mandrake – Maida leader answering – angels one-four – over' came Bottle's reply, rather curtly I thought, as if to give the impression to control that he was getting a bit fed up with him.

'Hallo Maida leader' cut in Mandrake again; Mandrake was now excited and talking fast, running away with himself, 'Very many bandits approaching bomb-dump from the south – repeat – very many bandits approaching bomb-dump from the south – gain angels as fast as you can – Buster – Buster – over to you – over.' 'OK Mandrake – your message received – we're doing our best – listening out' replied Maida leader. I looked at my code-card and identified 'Bomb-Dump' as being London. I thought how apt this was.

I switched on full oxygen and turned my trigger button on to 'Fire' at the same time adjusting my reflector-sight. At twenty-five thousand feet we entered the base of stratus cloud and closed up our formation to penetrate it. At twenty-seven thousand feet we were out of it. Above it the sun was brilliant as ever.

'Buster – Buster – Maida Squadron' – Mandrake kept calling. 'Get off the bloody air Mandrake, you stupid clot – what the bloody hell do you think we're doing?' Someone, I don't think it was Bottle, replied. There was silence over the ether after that for the time being.

Beneath us, as we reached thirty-thousand feet and leveled out, there was a flat carpet of cloud, pure white in the bright sunlight. Above us, apart from a few delicate and remote wisps of cirrus, the sky was an intense blue, the sort of blue you find on an artist's palette. Behind us and slightly to our starboard the sun was still high in the sky and was dazzling to look into. To the east the stratus cloud was beginning to disperse and we could see across the North Sea to the Dutch Islands. Visibility was limited only by the curvature of the Earth.

The entire firmament, the vault of the heavens, was revealed to us. It stretched from Lille and St Omer in the rolling plains of the Pas-de-Calais to the south, eastwards down the sandy coastline of Northern France, past Dunkirk to the Belgian frontier, beyond that to the Dutch Islands and past them to the faint line of the German coast, and up as far north as the Norfolk coast of our own country. Such was the panorama that confronted us as we levelled out five miles above the earth and higher than the highest mountain.

'Hallo Mandrake' Maida leader called. 'Maida Squadron now at angels three-zero – Bandits in sight – Tally Ho.' 'Well done, Maida leader – Good Luck – Good Luck – over to you,' Mandrake replied.

Yes, there they were all right. Very many bandits, too. The sky was full of black dots, which, from where we were at the moment, might have been anything; but we knew only too well what they were. They were coming from the south; squadron upon squadron, fleet upon fleet, an aerial Armada the size of which I don't suppose Jules Verne or even Wells had envisaged. The main body of them was below us by quite ten thousand feet, but above them as escort, winged the protective fighter screen proudly trailing their long white plumes of vapour.

Our position was somewhere over Surrey at the moment, and as we approached the enemy formations which were still some miles away, we saw our own fighters – the eleven group squadrons and some from twelve group in the Midlands coming up from the north. There seemed to be quite a number of us. They too were black dots, climbing in groups of twelve or thirty-six in wing formation. Most of them were Hurricanes.

The enemy appeared to be disposed in three distinct and separate groups each comprising a hundred or more bombers. Above each group were about fifty fighters – ME 109s, and ME 110s. The bombers were Heinkels, Dorniers and Junkers 88s.

'Line astern formation – Maida squadron,' ordered Maida leader. We took up our battle formations at once, with 'A' Flight in the order of Red, Yellow and White. There were two machines behind me and three in front. 'Come up into line abreast 'B' Flight' came the next order from Red one. When we had completed this change the squadron was disposed in two lines of six machines flying abreast and at a distance of about fifty yards between each Flight.

We were ready to attack. We were now in the battle area and three-quarters of an hour had elapsed since we had taken off.

The two bomber formations furthest from us were already being attacked by a considerable number of our fighters. Spitfires and Hurricanes appeared to be in equal numbers at the time. Some of the German machines were already falling out of their hitherto ordered ranks and floundering towards the earth. There was a little ack-ack fire coming up from somewhere on the ground although its paucity seemed pathetic and its effect was little more than that of a defiant gesture.

We approached the westermost bomber formation from the front port quarter, but we were some ten thousand feet higher than they were and we hadn't started to dive yet. Immediately above the bombers were some twin-engined fighters, ME 110s. Maida Leader let the formation get a little in front of us then he gave the order 'Going down now Maida aircraft,' turning his machine upside-down as he gave it. The whole of 'A' Flight, one after the other, peeled off after him, upside-down at first and then into a vertical dive.

When they had gone 'B' Flight followed suit. Ferdie and I turned over with a hard leftward pressure to the stick to bring the starboard wing up to right angles to the horizon, and some application to the port or bottom rudder pedal to keep the nose from rising. Keeping the controls like this, the starboard wing fell over until it was parallel to the horizon again, but upside-down. Pulling the stick back from this position the nose of my machine fell towards the ground and followed White one in front, now going vertically down on to the bombers almost directly below us. Our speed started to build up immediately. It went from three hundred miles per hour to four and more. White one in front, his tail wheel some distance below me but visible through the upper part of my windscreen, was turning his machine in the vertical plane from one side to the other by the use of his ailerons. Red Section had reached the formation and had formed into a loosened echelon to starboard as they attacked. They were coming straight down on top of the bombers, having gone slap through the protective ME 110 fighter screen, ignoring them completely.

Now it was our turn. With one eye on our own machines I slipped out slightly to the right of Ferdie and placed the red dot of my sight firmly in front and in line with the starboard engine of a Dornier vertically below me and about three hundred yards off. I felt apprehensive lest I should collide with our own machines in the *mêlée* that was to ensue. I seemed to see one move ahead what the positions of our machines would be, and where I should be in relation to them if I wasn't careful. I pressed my trigger and through my inch thick windscreen I saw the tracers spiralling away hitting free air in front of the bomber's engine; I was allowing too much deflection. I must correct. I pushed the stick further forward. My machine was past the vertical and I was feeling the effects of the negative gravity trying to throw me out of the machine, forcing my body up to the perspex hood of the cockpit. My Sutton harness was biting into my shoulders and blood was forcing its way to my head, turning everything red. My tracers were hitting the bomber's engine and bits of metal were beginning to fly off it. I was getting too close to it, much too close. I knew I must pull away but I seemed hypnotised and went still closer, fascinated by what was happening. I was oblivious to everything else. I pulled away just in time to miss hitting the Dornier's starboard wingtip. I turned my machine to the right on ailerons and heaved back on the stick, inflicting a terrific amount of gravity on to the machine. I was pressed down into the cockpit again and a black veil came over my eyes and I could see nothing.

I eased the stick a little to regain my vision and to look for Ferdie. I saw a machine, a single Spitfire, climbing up after a dive about five hundred yards in front of me and flew after it for all I was worth. I was going faster than it was and I soon caught up with it – in fact I overshot it. It was Ferdie all right. I could see the 'C' Charlie alongside our squadron letters on his fuselage. I pulled out to one side and back again hurling my machine at the air without any finesse, just to absorb some speed so that Ferdie could catch up with me. 'C' Charlie went past me and I thrust my throttle forward lest I should lose him. I got in behind him again and called him up to tell him so. He said: 'Keep an eye out behind and don't stop weaving.' I acknowledged his message and started to fall back a bit to get some room. Ferdie had turned out to the flank of the enemy formation and had taken a wide sweeping orbit to port, climbing fast as he did so. I threw my aircraft first on to its port wingtip to pull it round, then fully over to the other tip for another steep turn, and round again and again, blacking out on each turn. We were vulnerable on the climb, intensely so, for we were so slow.

I saw them coming quite suddenly on a left turn; red tracers coming towards us from the centre of a large black twin-engined ME 110 which wasn't quite far enough in the sun from us to be totally obscured, though I had to squint to identify it. I shouted to Ferdie but he had already seen the tracers flash past him and had discontinued his port climbing turn and had started to turn over on his back and to dive. I followed, doing the same thing, but the ME 110 must have done so too for the tracers were still following us. We dived for about a thousand feet, I should think, and I kept wondering why my machine had not been hit.

Ferdie started to ease his dive a bit. I watched him turn his machine on to its side and stay there for a second, then its nose came up, still on its side, and the whole aircraft seemed to come round in a barrel-roll as if clinging to the inside of some revolving drum. I tried to imitate this manoeuvre but I didn't know how to, so I just thrust open the throttle and aimed my machine in Ferdie's direction and eventually caught him up.

The ME 110 had gone off somewhere. I got up to Ferdie and slid once more under the doubtful protection of his tail and told him that I was there. I continued to weave like a pilot inspired, but my inspiration was the result of sheer terror and nothing more.

All the time we were moving towards the bombers; but we moved indirectly by turns, and that was the only way we could move with any degree of immunity now. Four Spitfires flashed past in front of us, they weren't ours, though, for I noticed the markings. There was a lot of talking going on on the ether and we seemed to be on the same frequency as a lot of the other squadrons. 'Hallo Firefly Yellow Section – 110 behind you' – 'Hallo Cushing Control – Knockout Red leader returning to base to refuel.' 'Close up Knockout 'N' for Nellie and watch out for those 109s on your left' – 'All right Landsdown Squadron – control answering – your message received – many more bandits coming from the east – over' – 'Talker White two where the bloody hell are you?' – 'Going down now Sheldrake Squadron – loosen up a bit' – 'You clumsy clot – Hurricane 'Y' Yoke – what the flaming hades do you think 'you are doing?' – 'I don't know Blue one but there are some bastards up there on the left – nine o'clock above' – Even the Germans came in intermittently: 'Achtung, Achtung – drei Spitfeuer unter, unter Achtung, Spitfeuer, Spitfeuer.' 'Tally Ho – Tally Ho – Homer Red leader attacking now' 'Get off the bastard air Homer leader' – 'Yes I can see Rimer leader – Red two answering – Glycol leak I think – he's getting out – yes he's baled out he's ok.'

And so it went on incessantly, disjointed bits of conversation coming from different units all revealing some private little episode in the great battle of which each story was a small part of the integral whole.

Two 109s were coming up behind the four Spitfires and instinctively I found myself thrusting forward my two-way radio switch to the transmitting position and calling out 'Look out those four Spitfires – 109s behind you – look out.' I felt that my message could hardly be of less importance than some that I had heard, but no heed was taken of it. The two 109s had now settled themselves on the tail of the rear Spitfire and were pumping cannon shells into it. We were some way off but Ferdie too saw them and changed direction to starboard, opening up his throttle as we closed. The fourth Spitfire, or 'tail-end Charlie', had broken away, black smoke pouring from its engine, and the third in line came under fire now from the same 109. We approached the two 109s from above their starboard rear quarter and, taking a long deflection shot from what must have been still out of range, Ferdie opened fire on the leader. The 109 didn't see us for he still continued to fire at number three until it too started to trail Glycol from its radiator and turned over on its back breaking away from the remaining two. 'Look out Black one – look out Black Section Apple squadron – 109s – 109s' came the belated warning, possibly from number three as he went down. At last number one turned steeply to port, with the two 109s still hanging on to their tails now firing at number two. They were presenting a relatively stationary target to us now for we were directly behind them. Ferdie's bullets were hitting the second 109 now and pieces of its tail unit were coming away and floating past underneath us. The 109 jinked to the starboard. The leading Spitfire followed by its number two had now turned full circle in a very tight turn and as yet it didn't seem that either of them had been hit. The 109 leader was vainly trying to keep into the same turn but couldn't hold it tight enough so I think his bullets were skidding past to the starboard of the Spitfires. The rear 109's tail unit disintegrated under Ferdie's fire and a large chunk of it slithered across the top surface of my starboard wing, denting the panels but making no noise. I put my hand up to my face for a second.

The fuselage of the 109 fell away below us and we came into the leader. I hadn't fired at it yet but now I slipped out to port of Ferdie as the leader turned right steeply and over on to its back to show its duck-egg blue belly to us. I came up almost to line abreast of Ferdie on his port side and fired at the under surface of the German machine, turning upside-down with it. The earth was now above my Perspex hood and I was trying to keep my sights on the 109 in this attitude, pushing my stick forward to do so. Pieces of refuse rose up from the floor of my machine land the engine spluttered and coughed as the carburettor became temporarily starved of fuel. My propellor idled helplessly for a second and my harness straps bit into my shoulders again. Flames leapt from the engine of the 109 but at the same time there was a loud bang from somewhere behind me and I heard 'Look out Roger' as a large hole appeared near my starboard wingtip throwing up the matt green metal into a ragged rent to show the naked aluminium beneath.

I broke from the 109 and turned steeply to starboard throwing the stick over to the right and then pulling it back into me and blacking out at once. Easing out I saw three 110s go past my tail in 'V' formation but they made no attempt to follow me round. 'Hallo Roger – Are you OK?' I heard Ferdie calling. 'I think so – where are you?' I called back.

'I'm on your tail – keep turning' came Ferdie's reply. Thank God, I thought. Ferdie and I seemed to be alone in the sky. It was often like this. At one moment the air seemed to be full of aircraft and the next there was nothing except you. Ferdie came up in 'V' on my port side telling me at the same time that he thought we had better try to find the rest of the squadron.

The battle had gone to the north. We at this moment were somewhere over the western part of Kent, and a little less than a quarter of an hour had elapsed since we had delivered our first attack on the bombers. Ferdie set course to the north where we could see in the distance the main body of aircraft. London with its barrage balloons floating unconcernedly, like a flock of grazing sheep, ten thousand feet above it, was now feeling the full impact of the enemy bombers. Those that had got through – and the majority of them had – were letting their bombs go. I recalled for an instant Mr Baldwin's prophecy, not a sanguine one, made to the House of Commons some five years before when he said that the bomber will always get through.

Now it was doing just that. I wondered if it need have done. As we approached South London the ground beneath us became obscured by smoke from the bomb explosions which appeared suddenly from the most unlikely sort of places an – open field, a house, a row of houses, a factory, railway sidings, all sorts of things. Suddenly there would be a flash, then a cloud of reddish dust obscuring whatever was there before and then drifting away horizontally to reveal once more what was left of the target.

I saw a whole stick of bombs in a straight line advancing like a creeping barrage such as you would see on the films in pictures like 'Journey's End' or 'All quiet on the Western Front', but this time they were not over the muddy desolation of No-Man's Land but over Croydon, Surbiton and Earl's Court. I wondered what the people were like who were fighting the Battle of Britain just as surely as we were doing but in a less spectacular fashion. I thought of the air raid wardens shepherding their flocks to the air raid trenches without a thought of their own safety; the Auxiliary Firemen and the regular fire brigades who were clambering about the newly settled rubble strewn with white-hot and flaming girders and charred wood shiny black with heat, to pull out the victims buried beneath; the nurses, both the professional ones and the VADs in their scarlet cloaks and immaculate white caps and cuffs, who were also clambering about the shambles to administer first aid to the wounded and give morphine to the badly hurt; the St John's Ambulance brigade who always were on the spot somehow no matter where or under what circumstances an accident or emergency occurred, helping, encouraging and uplifting the victims without thought for themselves; the Red Cross and all the civilian volunteers who, when an emergency arises, always go to assist. Not least I thought of the priests and clergy who would also be there, not only to administer the final rites to the dying but to provide an inspiration to those who had lost faith or through shock seemed temporarily lost. The clergy were there all right and showed that their job was not just a once-a-week affair at the Church, but that religion was as much a part of everyday living as was eating and sleeping.

I felt humble when I thought of what was going on down there on the ground. We weren't the only people fighting the Battle of Britain. There were the ordinary people, besides these I've mentioned, all going about their jobs quietly yet heroically and without any fuss or complaint. They had no mention in the press or news bulletins, their jobs were routine and hum-drum and they got no medals.

We were now in the battle area once again and the fighting had increased its tempo. The British fighters were becoming more audacious, had abandoned any restraint that they might have had at the outset, and were allowing the bombers no respite at all. If they weren't able to prevent them from reaching their target they were trying desperately to prevent them from getting back to their bases in Northern France. The air was full of machines, the fighters, British and German, performing the most fantastic and incredibly beautiful evolutions. Dark oily brown streams of smoke and fire hung vertically in the sky from each floundering aircraft, friend or foe, as it plunged to its own funeral pyre miles below on the English countryside. The sky, high up aloft, was an integrated medley of white tracery, delicately woven and interwoven by the fighters as they searched for their opponents. White puffs of ack-ack fire hung limply in mid-air and parachute canopies drifted slowly towards the ground.

It was an English summer's evening. It was about a quarter to six. We had been in the air now for about an hour and a quarter and our fuel would not last much longer. We had failed to join up with the rest of the flight, but this was understandable and almost inevitable under the circumstances. I don't suppose the others were in any formation other than sections now.

Beneath us at about sixteen thousand feet, while we were at twenty-three, there were four Dorniers by themselves still going north and I presumed, for that reason, they hadn't yet dropped their bombs. Ferdie had seen them and was making for them. Three Hurricanes in line astern had seen the same target, had overtaken them, turned, and were delivering a head-on attack in a slightly echeloned formation. It was an inspiring sight, but the Dorniers appeared unshaken as the Hurricanes flew towards them firing all the time. Then the one on the port flank turned sharply to the left, jettisoning its bomb load as it went. The leading Hurricane got on to its tail and I saw a sheet of flame spring out from somewhere near its centre section and billow back over the top surface of its wing, increasing in size until it had enveloped the entire machine except the extreme tips of its two wings. I didn't look at it any more.

We were now approaching the remaining three Dorniers and we came up directly behind them in line astern. 'Get out to port Roger' cried Ferdie 'and take the left one.' I slid outside Ferdie and settled my sight on the Dornier's starboard engine nacelle. We were not within range yet but not far off. The Dorniers saw us coming all right and their rear-gunners were opening fire on us, tracer bullets coming perilously close to our machines. I jinked out to port in a lightening steep turn and then came back to my original position and fired immediately at the gunner and not the engine. The tracers stopped coming from that Dornier. I changed my aim to the port engine and fired again, one longish burst and my 'De-Wilde' ammunition ran up the trailing edge of the Dornier's port wing in little dancing sparks of fire until they reached the engine. The engine exploded and the machine lurched violently for a second as if a ton weight had landed on the wing and then fallen off again for, as soon as the port wing had dropped it picked up again and the bomber still kept formation despite the damage to its engine. The engine was now totally obscured by thick black smoke which was being swept back on to my windscreen. I was too close to the bomber now to do anything but break off my attack and pull away. I didn't see what had happened to the Dornier that Ferdie had attacked and what's more I could no longer see Ferdie.

I broke off in a steep climbing turn to port scanning the sky for a single Spitfire – 'C' Charlie. There were lots of lone Spitfires, there were lots of lone Hurricanes and there were lots of lone bombers but it was impossible now and I thought improvident to attempt to find Ferdie in all this *mêlée*. I began to get concerned about my petrol reserves as we had been in the air almost an hour and a half now and it was a long way back to base.

I pressed my petrol indicator buttons and one tank was completely empty, the other registering twenty-two gallons. I began to make some hasty calculations concerning speed, time and distance and decided that if I set course for base now and travelled fairly slowly I could make it. I could put down at another airfield of course and get refuelled, but it might be bad policy, especially for a new pilot.

I called up Ferdie, thinking, not very hopefully, that he might hear me, and told him what I was doing. Surprisingly he came back on the air at once in reply and said that he was also returning to base and asked me if I thought I had got enough fuel. He said that he thought it ought to be enough and added as an after-thought that I should make certain that my wheels and flaps were working satisfactorily before coming too low, for they could be damaged. I thanked him for his advice and listened out. I was by myself now and still in the battle area and I was weaving madly for I realised how vulnerable I was. I was easy meat to German fighters, just their cup of tea, particularly if there should be more than one of them, for the Germans always seemed to fancy themselves when the odds were in their favour, particularly numerical odds. It was past six o'clock now and the sun was getting lower in the west, the direction I was travelling in. If I were going to be attacked from the sun, then it would be a head on attack. I felt fairly secure from behind, provided I kept doing steep turns.

I could see a single Spitfire in front of me and a little lower. It must be Ferdie, I thought at once, and chased after it to catch it up. It would be nice to go back to base together. When I got closer to it I noticed a white stream of Glycol coming away from underneath. There wasn't very much but it was enough to tell me that the machine had been hit in its radiator. It seemed to be going down on a straight course in a shallow dive. I got to within about three hundred yards of it and called up Ferdie to ask his position, feeling that he would be sure to tell me if he had been hit in the radiator, although he might not have wanted me to know in the first instance. I got no reply and for a second I became convinced that he had been attacked since I had last spoken to him. I opened up my throttle, although I ought to have been conserving my fuel. From the direct rear all Spitfires look exactly the same and I had to get up close to it to read the lettering. I came up on its port side and at a distance of about twenty yards. It wasn't Ferdie. I felt relief. It didn't belong to Maida Squadron at all. It was 'G' for George and belonged to some totally different squadron. I made a mental note of the lettering for 'Brain's' benefit. I closed in a bit to see what it was all about. The Glycol leak wasn't severe. I couldn't think what to make of it at all. Perhaps the pilot wasn't aware of the leak. Perhaps he had baled out already and the machine, as they have been known to, was carrying on alone, like the 'Marie Celeste'. Perhaps it was my imagination, an hallucination after the excitement and strain of the past hour. I came in very close to it as though I were in squadron formation and it no longer presented a mystery to me. The pilot was there, his head resting motionless against the side of the perspex hood. Where it was resting, and behind where it was resting, the perspex was coloured crimson. Now and then as the aircraft encountered a disturbance and bumped a little, the pilot's head moved forward and back again. The hood was slightly open at the front which gave me the impression that he had made an instinctive last minute bid to get out before he had died. The wind had blown into the cockpit and had blown the blood which must have gushed from his head, back along the entire length of the cockpit like scarlet rain. I became suddenly and painfully aware that I was being foolhardy to stay so close as this for a sudden reflex from the pilot, dead though he was, a sudden thrust of the rudder bar or a movement from the stick could hurl the aircraft at me. I swung out and left it. I didn't look back any more. Before I left it, it had started to dive more steeply, and the Glycol flowed more freely as the nose dipped and the speed increased.

I thanked God for many things as I flew back away from the din and noise of the battle through the cool and the peace of the evening across the New Forest and above Netley to base. I landed my machine at six-thirty, stepped out and went to the hut.

Brains was very much in evidence and busy collecting reports from different people. Most of the pilots had landed and Ferdie, I was glad to see, was among them. I gave my report to Brains and Ferdie checked it. I was granted two damaged aircraft and Ferdie got one confirmed and two damaged. There were still three of our pilots unaccounted for. P/O Watty was not down and Red two and Blue two were overdue. We were allowed up to the mess in parties of six at a time, for we were still on readiness until nine o'clock. Ferdie and I went together and discussed the events of the last hour or so. We had some supper and then went down to dispersal again to relieve the others. It was unlikely, I was told, that we should be scrambled again in any strength for it was getting late now and the Germans would hardly be likely to mount another large offensive as late as this.

Brains was still down in the hut and was spending most of his time at the telephone answering calls from Group Intelligence and making enquiries from other stations as to the possible fate of our, own missing pilots. Eventually news came through that Watty was safe but had been shot down near Southampton on his way back to base. He had been attacked by two ME 109s in this area and his machine had been hit in the Glycol tank but he had managed to force land. He was taken to the hospital there because the medical officer had found a rip in his tunic which, upon further investigation, had revealed that he had got some shrapnel of some sort into his arm. We heard later that Red two and Blue two had both been shot down and both of them had been killed. Blue two had gone down in flames in front of a ME 110 and Red two had pressed his attack too closely to a Heinkel 111 and had gone into it. Both of these were sergeant pilots.

The squadron, according to Brains' assessment, had accounted for eight confirmed aircraft, three probables and seven damaged. There was no further flying that day and we were released at nine o'clock. We went up to the mess as usual and after some drinks we got into our cars and left the camp. We were to rendezvous at the Sunray.

We got to the Sunray after five minutes or so. It wasn't far from the aerodrome and was tucked away at the end of a lane leading from the main Weymouth-Wareham road.

The Sunray was blacked out and it was pitch dark outside when we switched off our lights. We groped our way to the door which Chumley seemed able to find in some instinctive manner. He opened the front door calling to me 'Switch your radar on Roger' and pulled aside a blanket which had been rigged up to act as a further precaution to prevent the light from escaping as the main door was opened. We got inside to find the others already drinking. Cocky seemed to be in the chair as Chumley and I came in and he called out 'Lost again White Section – biggies coming up for both of you.'

The Sunray was an old pub and full of atmosphere. The ceilings were low and oak beams ran the entire length of them. In between the beams, the ceiling itself was made of wood of the same colour. It seemed dark at first but there was a liberal amount of lamps, not on the ceiling itself but on the walls, and these gave a soft light that was distinctly cosy. There were tables of heavy oak around which were chairs made out of barrels, highly polished and each containing soft plushy cushions. Around the walls ran an almost continuous cushion-covered bench, and the windows, from what I could see of them, for they were heavily curtained, were made of bottle-glass and were only translucent. The serving bar in the middle of the room was round and from it hung a varied assortment of brilliantly polished copper and brass ornaments. There were roses in copper vases standing on some of the tables and a bowl or two on the bar itself. There were sandwiches beneath glass cases and sausage-rolls as well. The visible atmosphere in the room was cloudy with tobacco smoke which seemed to reach its optimum height a foot or so from the ceiling where it appeared to flatten out and drift in horizontal layers until someone passed through it and then it appeared to follow whoever did so for a moment. There was a wireless somewhere in the room, for I could hear music coming from near where I was standing.

I was by the bar with the others and I had finished my third pint of bitter and was talking to Cocky. The night was quite early yet and Bottle was standing up at the bar with Dimmy, Chumley and Pete; they were all laughing at the top of their voices and a bit further along was Ferdie listening to what might, I think, have been a rather long-drawn-out story from one of the sergeant pilots, while two others seemed impatiently trying to get him to the point. Ferdie seemed to be quite amused at the process. There were two of our Polish pilots here too, both non-commissioned and their names were so difficult to pronounce that we simply called them 'Zig' and 'Zag'. They didn't seem to take any offence at this abbreviation. They were excellent pilots, both of them.

The wireless now started to play the theme of Tchaikovsky's 'Swan Lake' ballet and when I'd got my sixth pint I mentally detached myself from the rest for a moment.

'Wotcher Roger, mine's a pint of black and tan – have one yourself.' I was jolted back to reality by this, accompanied by a hearty slap on the back from Ferdie, who had wormed his way across to me.

I had my seventh pint with Ferdie and we both edged up closer to the bar where the main body of the squadron seemed to have congregated. It was Cocky who, high spirited and irrepressible as ever, said 'Come on boys, we've had this – next stop the Crown.' We picked up our caps and made for the door. 'Mind the light,' someone shouted as the protective blanket was thrust aside for a moment. The air outside was cold and it hit me like a cold shower for a brief second while I gathered my wits. Chumley piled into the passenger seat. I was feeling perhaps a little too self-confident after the drinks but I felt sure I would make it somehow.

We got on to the main road again and Chumley directed us to the Crown in Weymouth. The road was fairly free of traffic and I gave the little car full rein for a while. It was dark and just in front of me there seemed to be an even darker but obscure sort of shape which I found difficulty in identifying for a moment. 'For Christ's sake, man' Chumley shouted. Cocky's large Humber had pulled up on the verge and its occupants were busy relieving themselves by the roadside, but one of them was standing in front of the rear light and obscuring it. We were travelling at not much less than seventy-five mph when Chumley shouted at me and the Humber was only about thirty yards from us when I recognised it. My slow-wittedness only now became evident but I felt quite confident and in complete control of my faculties as I faced the emergency. I pulled the wheel over to the right, not abruptly but absolutely surely and with a calculated pressure to allow me only inches, inches enough to guide the left mud-guard past the Humber's off rear bumper. At the time I was in full control and thinking how fine and assured were my reactions, how much finer they were now than they ever were when I had had no drink. The sense of complete infallibility and the consequent denial of any risk had overtaken me and the feeling, if anything, became accentuated when the little car had passed Cocky's large Humber, which it did by the barest fraction of an inch, to an accompanying shout of 'Look out, 109s behind' from those who were standing by the verge and otherwise engaged. 'No road sense, those boys' Chumley remarked.

The Crown was quite a different sort of place from the Sunray. From the outside it was distinctly unpretentious in appearance, just a flat-sided building flanking the back street down by the harbour. It had four windows, two top and bottom and a door in the middle. We went in, and as I had rather expected, it was an ordinary working-man's pub. There were no furnishings to speak of, the floor was just plain wooden boards and the few tables were round with marble tops and the conventional china ash-trays advertising some type of lager or whisky. The bar occupied the whole of one side of the room and the barman greeted us warmly as we arrived. Chumley ordered two pints of bitter. Apparently the squadron were well-known and held in high esteem.

The others arrived soon after we got there and the drinks were on me this time. There was a dartboard in the corner of the room and, not surprisingly, we threw badly. What did it matter how we played I thought, as long as we let off some steam.

When we left the Crown at closing time I was drunk, but we didn't return to the aerodrome. Bottle had some friends in Bournemouth and it was to Bournemouth that he'd decided to go. I was too drunk to drive and so was Chumley, who had left the Crown before closing time and taken up his position in the passenger seat of my car where he was now fast asleep. Dimmy and I lifted him out, still asleep, into the back of Cocky's Humber. Dimmy, who, so he claimed, was more sober than I, said he would drive my car. I made no protest. I relapsed into the passenger seat and fell asleep as the car gathered speed towards Bournemouth. I woke up as soon as the car came to a standstill, feeling a lot more sober. It was about half-past eleven when we went through the door of this quite large private house. Bottle's and Cocky's car had already arrived and the occupants had apparently gone inside. The door opened and a girl greeted us. 'I'm Pam, come on in the others are here,' she said. Everyone was seated in or on some sort of chair or stool and all had a glass of some sort in their hand. There were two other girls there besides Pam.

I was beginning to feel rather tired about this time and I would have been glad to get back to camp, especially as I had to be on dawn readiness again. The atmosphere here didn't seem conducive to any sort of rowdery like the Crown or the Compass and the girls didn't somehow seem to fit into the picture. They weren't on the same wavelength. It was about two-thirty in the morning when we finally left.

We arrived back at the mess just after four o'clock, having stopped at an all-night cafe for eggs and bacon and coffee. I had to be on readiness at five-thirty and it seemed hardly worthwhile going to bed, so I decided to go straight down to dispersal, to find I was the only one there. I had just an hour and a half's sleep before I was due to take off on dawn patrol.

5

Angels Two-Zero: September 1940

We took off at six o'clock. We were Red Section, and as soon as we were in the air, Bottle called up control to say that Maida Red Section were now airborne. I was flying in port Vick of Bottle and was in quite loose formation. I felt much better now that I was in my machine once more. The heavy cloud that had obscured the sunlight an hour ago had now almost disappeared and as we continued climbing in an easterly direction we could see the remains of what must have been a gorgeous sunrise. The horizon itself was purple and the sky above the horizon was the same colour. Above this there were a few wisps of cirrus, brushed delicately with a vivid crimson, and above these were pieces of open sky, pure gold in colour. It was really beautiful. The gold gave way to yellow as it got higher and this in turn to pale green and finally to blue. Among the blue, much higher than we could ever go, was more cirrus, exquisite to gaze upon, golden cirrus, icily remote in the uppermost realm of the atmosphere.

The air was calm and quiet as it so often is at this time of day and our two Spitfires hummed easily along the air paths, not bumping or jolting at all but keeping station one with the other with no effort at all. The world of last night seemed a long way off, and I wondered how, by contrast to this ecstatic feeling I had now, I could ever have descended to the general debauchery which characterised last night's behaviour. I wondered what the alternatives were. Were we to sit in our rooms and read a book, or sit in the mess and do the crossword puzzle or read all about the war, or write letters to our loved ones in case we got no further opportunity, or should we go to the cinema? I didn't think any of these activities would really be adequate as a sequence to the events of the day.

It would be physically possible to sit down by oneself in one's room and read a book after fighting Germans at a great height and at great speed at intervals during the day – but it would be unnatural. I concluded, by a process of eliminating the alternatives, that I should either have to become unnatural and estrange myself from the squadron, or become a drunk by night. It was no longer a mystery to me why fighter pilots had earned such a reputation for being somewhat eccentric when they were on the ground. I knew why it was, and I knew that if I were alive this evening I should get drunk with the others and go wherever they went.

We were now over Portland harbour at twenty thousand feet and orbiting this position. Control had not called us during our ascent, which had taken us a little less than a quarter of an hour.

We continued to orbit in a wide circle the diameter of which, when related to the ground, stretched from Dorchester through Weymouth to some five or six miles south of the Portland peninsular. I was still in 'V' formation with Bottle for there seemed to be no immediate cause for me to get into line astern and start weaving. If I had said this to anyone at the time I should have immediately evoked from them the comment 'famous last words', which was intended to prevent a state of over-confidence.

'Hallo Maida Red one – Mandrake calling – are you receiving me?' 'Hallo Mandrake – Red one answering – receiving you loud and clear – over.' 'Hallo Maida Red one – Mandrake answering – receiving you loud and clear also – I may have some information for you shortly

– continue to orbit your position – Mandrake to Maida leader over.' 'Hallo Mandrake, Red leader answering – your message received and understood – continuing to orbit – listening out.' I don't suppose we had been in the air for more than half an hour when this message came through and I can't say that it meant very much to me when it did. I expect it meant something to Bottle. He would probably connect it with events which had followed messages of a similar nature before, but he showed no sign of alarm. Bottle from this distance, about fifty yards I should think, might have been anyone sitting there in his cockpit. His helmet gave him a certain anonymity. He seemed to be doing nothing in particular, but just sitting there in the cockpit of his 'A' for Arthur. If it had been possible to smoke, I'm sure that Bottle would have been puffing away contentedly, elegantly tapping the ash from a cigarette held in its holder into some convenient receptacle, probably the map-case. Such was his composure that I don't suppose he would have bothered to remove the cigarette from his mouth even during a dogfight with half a dozen 109s. Of course this is only conjecture, for one cannot smoke in a single engined aircraft with any degree of safety. The petrol tank and the fumes from it are just in front of you and fumes are highly volatile. Apart from this, one has one's oxygen mask continually on one's face and even if the aircraft is not high enough to warrant having to use oxygen it is necessary to wear it, for the radio-transmitter is incorporated in it. If these limitations did not exist I'm quite certain that Bottle would smoke and I'm dead certain I would all the time.

'Hallo Maida Red leader – Mandrake calling, Vector 090 – Vector 090 degrees – over.' 'Hallo Mandrake, Red leader answering – your message received and understood – 090 degrees it is – listening out.' We set off due east, still maintaining our height of angels twenty. Due east would take us south of Swanage, across Poole Harbour, and up the Solent if we kept on this course. I thought immediately of Southampton. Most of the scrambles for the squadron had been to the Southampton area except those for the London battles.

'Hallo Maida Red leader – Mandrake calling – increase your angels to two-five – there is one bandit approaching 'Bandstand' at angels two-zero from the south – Mandrake to Red leader, over.' 'Hallo Mandrake, Red leader answering – understand angels two-five, your message received listening out.'

Looking at my code card for the day I saw that 'Bandstand' was Southampton, which was rather what I had expected. One bandit at this time of day, so the others had told me, was most certainly a reconnaissance plane either photographing the previous night's raid damage or assessing the suitability of the weather conditions for a raid today or possibly both.

Bottle pulled the nose of his machine up in what I thought was a particularly perilous angle but who was I to say? My airspeed dropped to 120 mph or less and my climb indicator passed the three thousand feet a minute mark. Apart from Bottle's machine on my left, I saw only the sky and wisps of cirrus, now turned silver, high above us. Despite all our vaunted technical mastery we were no match for the cirrus nor would we be for some years to come. We were but insects which had just learnt to leave the ground, angrily scratching about on the earth's boundary layer. We took just over five minutes to get up to our new altitude, and flattened out immediately we got there.

'Hallo Mandrake, Maida leader calling – we are now at angels two-five have you any further information for us? over.' 'Hallo Maida leader – Mandrake answering – your message received – no further information – continue on your present course – over.'

Looking down for a minute I could see the white pointed tops of the needles as they rose out of a layer of mist covering the sea. The Isle of Wight was only partly visible beyond them. The horizon was indistinct and it was difficult to distinguish the sea from the sky, for the whole of the distant background was a sort of slate grey with no apparent depth or perspective to it. Vertically beneath us however, visibility was good. We were now over the Solent and Bottle called up control once more to ask for further instructions. Control told us to orbit our position. We did so.

It was wonderful up there and flying conditions were perfect. We were in a different world, a new world. I felt as though the world of last night had been just make-believe, a two-dimensional world, where little people think that they are bigger than they are, and in so doing become smaller. I wondered if it were possible to feel depressed in this new world and I thought that psychiatrists and mental quacks might be well advised to inaugurate a course of flying therapy to add to their many other therapies.

'Hallo Maida leader – Mandrake calling, Bandit is now just south of Battleship – angels two-zero – you should see it very soon – Mandrake to Maida leader, over.' 'Battleship', according to the code card, was the Isle of Wight, I looked in its direction but could see nothing.

'Hallo Mandrake, Maida leader answering – your message received and understood – can't see it yet – will keep you informed – listening out,' Bottle replied. 'Better get into line astern Red two' he continued, speaking to me. I acknowledged his order and slid my machine into position behind him, keeping some distance away. I searched feverishly for any sign of the bandit. I suppose I had instinctively conjured up in my mind the shape of the bandit, I thought it would be a Junkers 88, the others had said that the 'Recce' planes were usually these. Suddenly I did see it, almost exactly as I had expected. It was a Junkers 88 and it was flying almost due north and seemed to be going very fast. At once I called to Bottle 'Hallo, Red leader – Red two calling – there it is – below at three o'clock – over.' 'OK, Roger, I see it, thanks,' came his reply. Bottle called up control and Tally ho'd. Control seemed satisfied with what they considered was their interception and bid us *bon voyage*.

Bottle waited until the German machine had gone past us underneath before going down on it. When it had crossed the Hampshire coast just west of Calshot he said 'All set, Roger? keep well out behind me.' I just replied 'OK Red one.' Bottle turned his machine over on to its back and I followed in the same style. My sights were on and so was my firing button. When I was upside-down I saw Bottle's 'A' for Arthur through the top of my hood going down vertically towards the Hampshire panorama, but for the moment I had lost sight of the Junkers 88.

I wasn't concerned with it, but only with sticking close to 'A' for Arthur. I pulled the stick hard back into my stomach to get my machine into a vertical attitude as quickly as possible. The engine spluttered and threatened to stop but soon caught itself again and I was now following 'A' for Arthur and travelling at over four hundred mph My controls stiffened up and my ear drums became painful for a minute until I could swallow. I could see the bandit now and it had apparently become aware of our presence too, for it had turned in a wide arc to port and was obviously shedding quite a bit of its altitude at the same time, for it was going at an enormous speed. The Junkers 88 was now going almost due west towards Poole but we were coming down on it rapidly. I was thrilled. The excitement of the chase consumed me and something of the great speed of the moment seemed to infuse itself into my thinking and feeling. I was no longer an ordinary mortal, I was a god. I had the fire power of an infantry battalion at my fingertips and the speed of thirteen hundred horses in my gloved left hand. Nothing could stop the leaden wall that I was soon to unleash and nothing could stem it or stand in one piece before it. What rubbish I was thinking, but that's how it was.

Bottle's 'A' for Arthur started to flatten out below me and I accordingly heaved back on my own stick and disappeared into the night of a sustained blackout and could see nothing. I kept it like this until I felt I was level and then eased the stick forward a little. The black veil dropped from beneath my eyes to reveal 'A' for Arthur just about twenty yards in front of me and not more than two hundred yards behind the Junkers 88. Bottle must be firing I thought, he was well within range. Yes, he was. I could see the tell-tale spirals of cordite and tracer leaving his machine and going straight into the target. The Junkers 88's, port engine was on fire already and was leaving behind a plume of black smoke which was now describing a shallow 'U' shape as the machine itself turned to port. We too turned to port and as we did so I could see tracers coming away from its rear-gun but they were quite innocuous for they were going yards to our starboard. The Junkers 88 now turned into a steep tight turn to port and the rear-gunner stopped firing. I supposed that he had blacked out for a minute. We followed and Bottle opened fire again on the turn, giving, I suspect, a lot of deflection to his aim. I hadn't fired yet but was becoming impatient to do so. We were turning inside the German machine's arc and it must have realised that it couldn't out-turn us.

The black smoke from its engine was starting to get in our way as we had to turn through it. We were very close to it and I could at times smell its pungent vapour. It smelled foreign. We continued to turn until at length the Junkers 88 turned completely over on its back and after describing a hundred and eighty degrees on its longitudinal axis now faced the opposite way. It started to pull away to starboard in a contrary steep turn but Bottle had whipped 'A' for Arthur on to its starboard wingtip with the rapidity of a striking cobra and his tracers were now pouring into the German aircraft's starboard engine nacelle. I was still behind Bottle and utterly fascinated by his demonstration. Flames, with a little accompanying smoke burst from the starboard engine and the machine levelled out of its turn as if to say that it had had enough. There certainly didn't seem much else it could do under these circumstances.

We had lost a lot of height since this somewhat uneven dogfight had begun but I hadn't noticed it while it was happening. We were down now to about eleven thousand feet and were somewhere over the Isle of Wight. The Junkers 88 had started to go into a slow spin and was going down vertically towards the sea. 'That seems to have done it,' I heard Bottle say, 'I think we will follow it down to make sure,' he added. We spiralled slowly down after the bandit, keeping a respectful distance from it in case the rear-gunner in a final act of defiance should feel inclined to hit back at us before he snuffed it.

'Why the hell don't you get out, you clots,' I thought aloud, 'you can't all be dead.' Someone ought to have baled out by now, surely. I kept my eyes on the machine the whole time, expecting to see black figures trailing white canopies jump away from it. The machine was still spinning and the spin seemed to become more vicious and faster the lower it came. I wondered how long a comparatively large aircraft could stand this before something snapped. I thought perhaps the crew, if there were any alive, were being prevented from getting out by the centrifugal force that must be exerting itself on them. I could imagine the panic that must have prevailed among them if this was so as the altitude ran out on them. I felt sorry for them. At five thousand feet the aircraft's port wing came off and hovered for a moment almost stationary in the airflow of the bomber and then started to fall like a leaf. 'It won't get home like that, I don't think,' I heard Bottle say in a rather laconic tone. If it had not been so entirely tragic and had no lives been involved, the whole episode might have been almost amusing, especially when Bottle enlivened the drama with a little wit.

As soon as the wing had fallen off the remainder of the aircraft stopped spinning and almost immediately two figures became separated from it, their parachutes as yet unopened, trailing behind them. They hadn't got much further to fall, but I thought they would be all right if their parachutes were good ones. The body of the aircraft hit the water with an enormous splash and at once a white spume of spray rose out of it, hung for a second and cascaded back on to it, settling itself into a white circle about the remains of the Junkers 88, which still floated on the surface. One of the parachutes had billowed out and the little figure on the ends of the shroud lines started to oscillate from side to side, his legs kicking the air as if to stop this. The other man was not so fortunate; he was still falling fast towards the sea, and still trailing behind him was the white unopened canopy. The air seemed to refuse to unfold the pleats. Maybe the body, for body it would soon be, was twisting to such an extent that the canopy was becoming twisted too so that the air could not get into it. The body and the canopy hit the sea together, and again a small spume of water rose to mark the spot and again it fell and covered both. The sea had exacted its toll. We circled over the spot only feet above the water and there was blood on it and among the blood – German blood, but even so human blood – there were bits of a German flying suit.

Bottle called me up to say 'One confirmed, I think, Roger,' and I agreed, but could not feel quite so light-hearted about it as he was. Bottle was used to this sort of thing by now, and I wondered if I should ever get used to it. We started to climb up and when we had got to two thousand feet called up Mandrake to tell them what had happened and also to say that one German aircrew was floating in the Solent at a certain spot and that it would probably be appreciated by the airman in question if some form of rescue were sent. We needn't have worried, for rescue boats were already racing towards the position. The whole of our battle had been witnessed from the coast.

Control seemed pleased with Maida Red Section and congratulated us as we flew to base. We landed at seven fifteen. When we got back inside the hut Brains, inevitably, was there waiting for us. He was looking a bit dishevelled, and had obviously been summoned from his bed at an unaccustomed hour, for he had a roll-top pullover on instead of a collar and tie, the pilot's privilege, and he had certainly not shaved.

'Wotcher Brains … One Junkers 88 confirmed … positions somewhere in the Solent, time … five past seven … number of bursts, three, range … two hundred yards shortening to fifty … two occupants baled out … one dead … the other now in the process of being rescued … anything else you want to know, Brains?' queried Bottle after giving this highly colourful account of our combat to the all-inquiring Intelligence. Brains was not impressed by this version and demanded it all over again. Bottle was always baiting Brains. He took his 'Mae-West' off, took out his cigarette case, put a cigarette into its holder, lit it, got on to his bed, inhaled deeply and said 'Come and sit on the bed and I'll tell you all about it, Brains.' Bottle was as cool as ever; his hands were not shaking as he fingered the long cigarette holder, I noticed. Mine always seemed to shake a bit after flying, whether we had been in action or not. I had not yet acquired that composure essential to an airman. Sooner or later I should just have to if I were to go on flying, or I should quickly become a nervous wreck.

At eight o'clock the whole of 'B' Flight came to readiness and Bottle and I were released to the mess for breakfast. The dawn readiness section normally didn't have to come back to dispersal until after lunch unless there was a major flap on, and so I was able to look forward to a comparatively civilised sort of morning.

I sat in the mess all the morning and read the papers and felt quite relieved to be able to do so. At half-past twelve I had lunch and went down to dispersal to relieve two of the others at one o'clock.

When I got down there 'B' Flight were getting ready to come up to lunch and the remainder of 'A' Flight were coming to readiness. There were Cocky, Ferdie, Sgt Woolton, myself, Dudley and Boy Mars to comprise the 'A' Flight readiness sections. At a quarter past one Red Section were scrambled to angels twenty over Portland. Dudley was leading and Boy Mars was his number two. This was the first scramble of the morning. There had been no flying at all, though the weather had been lovely.

The sun was hot outside and the remainder of the Flight were enjoying its heat sitting in deckchairs up against the side of the hut. I was dozing and both Ferdie and Sgt Woolton were reading. Cocky was giving his dog 'Pooch' a hip bath in an enamel basin. I was trying to sleep but I could do no more than doze. Perhaps I should have had a dog to whom I could periodically give a hip-bath in an enamel basin if only to take my mind off other things. Perhaps I should have had a girl whom I could go to visit instead of drinking after we were released at night. Perhaps I would go to see Anne again. I hadn't seen her now for almost a year and we hadn't written to each other for some time. I decided that it would be quite a good idea to get in touch and resolved to ring her up that evening and find out what she felt about it. I must confess that I had given little thought to her or for that matter any other girl since I had started flying. Flying had so totally absorbed me that I felt quite adequate without the opposite sex. In a purely selfish sort of way I had come to regard her now as unnecessary. I was still in love with her but I didn't think anything could possibly come of our association for her mother was quite adamant upon the subject of our ever getting married. I think Anne herself also wanted things to be that way, although she had said when we last met, that she was not certain. She never seemed to be certain. I would ring her up tonight, anyhow.

At about half-past two, over an hour after Blue Section had been scrambled, Cocky broke the silence by shouting 'For Christ's sake, off the deck 'A' Flight.' I was hurled out of my uneasy stupor back into reality. I had no need to ask the reason why 'A' Flight should be off the deck, for a little way off was a formation of almost a hundred German bombers about fifteen thousand feet up, headed in the direction of the aerodrome. The four of us rushed to our aircraft. I rushed to mine with precious little heroism, I'm afraid. I didn't see myself as a St George about to take off to slay the dragon but merely as someone who considered that there would be less danger in the air than on the ground when the bombs started to fall. Why had we not been scrambled ages ago, I wondered as I got into my aircraft, and what the hell had Red Section got up to. Perhaps they had been shot down. But this was no time for conjecture. We must get off the ground as quickly as possible. Cocky and Sgt Woolton as Yellow Section took off first as soon as they had taxied into position and I was frantically awaiting Ferdie's arrival as my leader, White one. Ferdie's machine seemed difficult to start, from what I could see. It would happen now of all times. His propeller was turning but the engine refused to fire. I started to feel panic as the bomber formation drew closer to the aerodrome and I tried to calculate the position from which they would release their bombs in order to hit it. It must be soon now. I tried to repress the impulse to take off without him and orbit the aerodrome to wait for him, and just managed to do so, but I resolved to take off whatever happened if I saw the bombs leave the bomb-bays of the enemy machines, feeling that I should just be able to get airborne before they reached the ground. The bombers were overhead now and still their bombs hadn't been released. If they were going to bomb the aerodrome it was too late now, they would have to make another turn over it. It was evident that they were not going to, for they were well past it now and going northwards. I suppose it was just a coincidence that they had been right over us at all. The oil temperature of my machine was getting dangerously high, as it always did when the engine idles on the ground. I opened up the engine to get some wind into the oil cooler if possible, but it seemed to get even hotter. At last Ferdie started his engine and without further ado was coming hell for leather towards me. I hoped his brakes would work.

As soon as he had turned into the wind he opened up, giving me a cursory wave as he did so. I followed in starboard 'V' formation. We got off the ground in no time at all and as soon as our wheels were retracted Ferdie turned his machine sharply to port in a climbing turn towards the north. 'Hallo Maida Yellow one ... where the hell are you ... White one calling,' I heard Ferdie calling. 'Hallo, Ferdie ... Yellow one answering ... due north of base ... angels four climbing like a flipping thunderbolt ... pull your finger out, White Section' Cocky replied. It struck me at the time that thunderbolts fell to earth, but I let it pass. We were traveling at full throttle and climbing at nearly three thousand feet a minute in the general direction of the enemy formation, which was just visible high up above and in front of us. I could see Yellow Section in front and above us also, going at full boost. Black streams of petrol vapour were coming away from both their engines. 'Better use your energy boost, Roger,' Ferdie called out to me, as he started to increase speed himself.

The makers stipulated that the emergency boost must not be used for more than five consecutive minutes, but now the occasion seemed to warrant the risk. I throttled back, pushed the red half-lever fully forward and then opened up the main throttle again. Immediately the aircraft seemed to leap forward with a jolt, hitting me in the back as it did so, and the engine started to vibrate – black smoke pouring out of each exhaust port. The engine vibration transmitted itself to the entire aircraft and I began to appreciate the maker's instructions. The strain on the engine must have been phenomenal. I opened my radiator to its fullest extent to try to cool it a bit, for the Glycol temperature was rising rapidly and threatening to pass the danger mark. We were gaining on Yellow Section, who, in turn, were getting up to the level of the bombers. Control, for the first time since we had taken off, came up on the air and made some quite unnecessary remark to which Cocky replied pretty curtly.

'Pull your fingers out, Mandrake. What the bloody hell are you playing at? Get off the air, I can see them, you boys should learn to keep awake, stupid clots.' Control had certainly slipped up badly here. We should have been scrambled long before the bombers had got anywhere near the English coast. However, there was nothing to be gained by acrimony now. It was quite clear what we had to do and we were trying desperately to do it. We reached the level of the bomber formation after about twenty minutes and levelled out at sixteen thousand feet behind and to their starboard. There were about eighty bombers dispersed in ten rows of eight machines each and stepped up from front to rear. At about five thousand feet above the formation there were another twenty ME 109s as escort, flying in two lines of ten, line astern of each other. They were making vapour trails. The enemy formation was about halfway between the English and Bristol Channels when we gained their altitude. Yellow and White Sections had now formed up in line astern and we were starting to overhaul the German formation when Cocky called up and said 'OK, chums, prepare for head-on attack.' I wondered how Cocky was going to lead us into this lot for it would have been suicide to have attacked them from the rear in the face of a co-ordinated battery of rear-guns. I put my goggles on and opened my sliding hood. I hadn't bothered to do this before when going into action although it was advised at OTU, mainly to facilitate the baling-out process and as a precaution against splinters from the windscreen or hood. I did it this time for I had no illusions about my chances of survival against this lot. There were only four of us and I began to feel respect for the law of averages.

Despite this I was still optimistic. I was a bit vague about the break-away procedure following a head-on attack, in fact I had never discussed the subject with anyone, feeling that when it came to the point, it would work itself out. I was at the rear of our formation and black smoke continued to pour out of my engine and I could smell it as it swept past my open cockpit. I had been using my emergency boost for twice the permitted length of time now but I wasn't caring much about the possible effects of this any more.

We were about three miles in front of the bombers when Cocky led us into them with a steep turn to port. I prayed very earnestly as we turned, and placed my right thumb on the firing button. I remember thinking my goggles seemed a bit misty as I slid out to echelon starboard of Ferdie as we completed our turn and were now heading straight for the enemy formation. I opened fire immediately, not aiming at any machine in particular, but at the whole target. It was a compact target, a great juggernaut of metal flying extremely close together and it was difficult to see daylight between the individual machines. The fighter escort above were still in station and had not molested us yet. The four of us were in a shallow echelon to starboard and in good relative formation, being fairly steady and all firing together. Thirty-two machine guns firing at the rate of thirteen hundred rounds a minute for each gun were hitting something, somewhere about that target. We had only seconds in which to fire for we were approaching each other at a speed of not much less than six hundred mph. I was watching for the results of our fire during those brief seconds but could see none. From the corner of my eye I saw Cocky turn his machine on to its port wing and go down beneath the leading rank of the bombers, followed immediately by Yellow two, and then Ferdie started the turn, but being at the rear of the echelon I hadn't done so yet. I thought there was a little more time in which to hit the bombers. I was wrong for I pushed up my goggles from my eyes for a second and saw the sort of thing that one sees only in nightmares or aerial fighting. I was about to collide with the leading bomber of the front row. All I was conscious of was the perspex nose section of a Heinkel 111 coming straight at me. It seemed as though a single frame of a cinema film had stopped dead as they do when the projector breaks down.

I was in total darkness at once and my body seemed to contract into itself like a concertina. I was certain that I wasn't going to get away with this. If I wasn't going to hit an enemy machine, then the wings of my aircraft were going to come off with the force of the 'G' I was exerting on them. I felt a jolt round about my tail section and I thought that I must have hit it against some part of the bomber and I awaited the consequences. There didn't seem to be any. I still couldn't see anything and my hands were like ton weights on the controls. My aircraft shuddered for a moment. It was a stall shudder. Then the machine whipped round into a spin and I could see again. I could see the ground turning round beneath the nose of my aircraft. The English countryside was going round and with it some barrage balloons above a town. I didn't mind this happening. Nothing seemed to register with me and the aircraft just continued to spin and I made no effort to stop it. My thumb was still pressed on the trigger on the control column and intermittently bursts of fire came from my gun ports, the bullets presumably burying themselves somewhere in the English fields below. I looked at my altimeter and it registered only eight thousand feet. I had lost quite a lot of height during this semi-coma of mine. I felt distinctly shaken and started to take corrective action to recover from the spin which I was still in. I was spinning to port and so I pushed forward the starboard rudder pedal and the spin slowed up until it stopped, but I didn't remove the pressure on the pedal when it stopped and the machine whipped into another but contrary spin to starboard. This spin was faster and more vicious than the first and I applied the opposite rudder to stop it. The machine began to spin more slowly, until it stopped, but my reactions were too slow and again I didn't release the pressure of my foot on the rudder pedal in time, so the machine again whipped over into another spin to port. It spun faster than the last time and even more viciously. What was the matter with me? Had I forgotten how to fly? I thought the tail unit had been damaged possibly. Perhaps I had touched one of the bombers after all. I looked round at it to see if it was all in one piece, and it appeared to be. The ground was getting nearer.

It was now three thousand feet off and I made a supreme effort to pull myself together. I must be suffering from some sort of psychological shock, and my reactions had become clumsy. There was nothing wrong with the machine, I had assured myself of that. It was human frailty that was at fault. I pulled myself together, got the aircraft out of its spin and let it continue its dive for a bit to rid itself of any further tendency to stall. When it had recovered flying speed, I pulled the machine up into its level position and found my altimeter reading two thousand feet.

I felt horribly shaken and I just flew around aimlessly for a while to try to regain some sort of self-confidence. I thanked God for many things. I looked about the sky for the others and for the battle but both of these seemed to have passed over and gone. No one else seemed to be in the sky. I realised at once what I must do. If I didn't conquer myself now while I was in a state not far removed from cowardice, then I never would. I should eke out the remainder of my life in a state of nervous apprehension in some sort of institution, and the horror of the leading Heinkel would remain indelibly imprinted upon my mind for ever. I must get back to the battle wherever it was and suffer other experiences which would serve to expunge from my mind the one through which I had just passed.

I started to climb towards the north and immediately began to feel very alone and vulnerable. I also felt very foolhardy. There was no cover, there were no clouds of any sort and the glare from the sun was intense. A few moments before there had been a lot of enemy fighters about me and I could see no reason why there should not be now. A climbing machine labouring slowly up a steep incline is an easy target and an almost impotent opponent. It cannot turn suddenly without stalling, it cannot even manoeuvre without losing precious altitude, and of course the sun is a menace. Unless its camouflage is perfect, and that depended on what the ground beneath it was like, it was an easy-eye-catcher for a lookout flying above.

I was alone in the battle area for the first time. It was entirely up to me what I did now. I could fly straight back to base if I liked. It was so easy to turn back under such conditions. No one could see, no one could gainsay what I would say by way of explanation; technical failure, lack of ammunition, oxygen failure, wireless indistinct, engine overheating. One could invent a host of lies to save oneself from further immediate danger. Why bother to be brave, why stick one's neck out further than was necessary.

Suddenly I was aware and enormously conscious of the real significance of God in my life, and I was alone no longer.

My immediate goal was to regain my altitude. I did this and flattened out, increasing speed as I did so. Self-confidence seemed to flow back into me as I threw my aircraft about the open spaces of the sky, challenging it to do its worst. I could see no sign of the others or for that matter anyone else, German or British. The sky seemed empty, and after some minutes I called up to say that I was returning to base.

I landed to find the other three of our two sections already down and they were amazed to see me when I came into the hut. Cocky said by way of greeting 'Well, if it's not Roger the rammer himself, I thought you were after getting yourself a posthumous VC or something. Why didn't you break below with Ferdie?' he asked. I felt like crying with joy for a moment, then I did my best to explain what had happened, assuring him that my apparent bravado was entirely involuntary and at best could only be described as the result of being a clumsy clot. Cocky had shot a Heinkel 111 down in flames over Bristol, which the formation had bombed, and Ferdie and Sgt Woolton had both claimed a Junkers 88 each as destroyed. 'B' Flight had taken off about ten minutes after we had and the CO had got one enemy machine but had been hit in his petrol tank by something and had crash-landed near Yeovil. In all, the squadron had been credited with five confirmed and three probables. We had lost two pilots, one sergeant pilot and one flying officer from 'B' Flight – both killed.

6

Tail-End Charlie: September 1940

The following night I went to see Anne. She was living with friends at a small place just outside Marlborough. The journey was about sixty miles, but distance seemed to have very little meaning for me. I couldn't leave until we were released by operation HQ and at this time it was seldom before nine o'clock. By the time I had changed and had had dinner in the mess it was not far off ten.

I set off in the little car which was amply supplied with 100 octane aircraft fuel, a practice none of us who owned cars had many scruples about. Since pool petrol was rationed, I had to cash in on this 'amenity'. Although the authorities knew it was contrary to regulations, they suffered it in a diplomatic silence that helped to preserve a harmony between air crews and their austere brothers in the Provost branch.

The route to Marlborough was for the most part a long straight road across undulating plains which at this time of the night were almost deserted. I used to travel normally at speeds of little less than 70 mph which would have appeared incredible in view of the limited range of the masked headlights then in use, but I also had a foglight that I kept on the whole time, although it was forbidden except when it was foggy.

I arrived at Anne's place at eleven-thirty and found her dressed simply in a Hungarian type skirt, a white blouse and red sandals. She seemed genuinely pleased to see me and there was a lot we had to say to each other. We hadn't been together for over a year now and this, I must confess, was because I had felt in such little need of her. Flying had satisfied all my emotions and had employed all my faculties. When the prospect of sudden extinction became more than a remote possibility I was, as were many others, brought face to face with a desire to get married and to fulfil the laws of nature in order that something of me might remain when I was just a piece of charred humanity lying beneath a burnt-out aeroplane.

That was why I asked Anne to marry me. It was not the only reason, of course, because I was still very much in love with her and I had every reason to believe my love was reciprocated.

However, she was undecided, and I think was very much influenced by her mother, who disapproved of me not so much as a person as because I was a close relative. Perhaps she was right, but I considered her attitude unreasonable, with the result that my visits to Anne became increasingly unpopular so far as her mother was concerned.

There was no interference the first time I went to see her. We stayed together until three in the morning and she cooked me eggs and bacon before seeing me off from the gate in the raw chilliness before dawn. As I waved goodbye to her – a pathetic and somewhat lonely figure shivering in the cold – I cursed myself for not having tried to see her more often. I could never forget how she had given me the love of which I was in such dire need after leaving hospital, and without which I would never have recovered sufficiently to be able to join the RAF.

I drove back in a daze, hardly able to control the car and half believing I was already married to her. At the same time, I wondered how marriage would affect my flying. I had been told many times that fighter pilots who got married often lost much of their former aggressiveness and, by the time

I reached my station, I was half convinced that it would be better to remain single, at least for the time being.

I managed to snatch three hours' sleep and woke up at eight when the rest of the Flight came on duty, to find it pouring with rain. 'Wakey wakey! Rise and shine! Go and get your big eats!' shouted Cocky, as he spotted me still nestling beneath the blankets.

'No flying this morning, boys,' Chumley said, squatting on one of the beds and picking up a copy of *Lady Chatterley's Lover.* 'Now at last I'll have a chance to read this flaming book.'

'Tell Ops the Nizam of Hyderabad's squadron will not be flying today, Corporal,' Cocky called out jestingly to the telephone operator who, in an effort to get the gist of his instruction, said, 'Shall I tell 'em that the pilots say there's no lift in the air when it's wet, sir?'

'No. Tell them that the aircraft have gone soggy standing outside and they'd better send us some hangars pretty bloody smart.'

Ten minutes later, just as I was boarding the truck, Cocky appeared at the door of the hut and shouted, 'Hey, come back! Squadron to readiness – squadron to readiness – very many bandits approaching base – take cover – take cover – !' At first I thought he was serious but then I didn't know Cocky as well as some of the others did. As the penny dropped and I started off for the truck again, someone said, 'One of these days he'll cry wolf once too often and then there'll be a shambles, by Christ there will.'

I had breakfast and read the papers. I didn't have to be at dispersal until after lunch so I decided to go back to my room, have a shave and get some more sleep in. I woke up at about twelve and it had stopped raining. There were a few broken bits of dark cloud drifting rapidly westwards, but in between them there was plenty of blue sky showing. I couldn't complain. I had been able to make up for my loss of sleep and I felt able to cope with whatever was to come.

Above left: 1. Roger on the wing of his Spitfire.
Above right: 2. On 8 August 1940 152 Squadron went into action to defend Convoy 'Peewit' in the English Channel. During the action this Spitfire, flown by Sergeant Denis Robinson was shot down by Messerschmitt Bf 109s. Robinson crash landed at Marsh Farm, Bestwall, Wareham, Dorset and walked away unhurt.

3. Roger in the cockpit.

4, 5, 6 & 7. Roger, *top left*, in his flying helmet, *top right*, sporting his DFC.

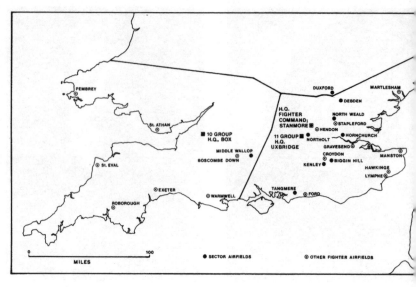

8. Map of RAF bases 1940.

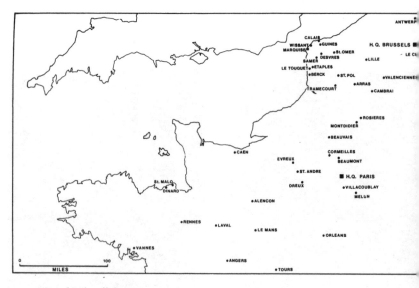

9. Map of Luftwaffe bases 1940.

10. Roger in his new MG, August 1940.

11. Roger with his brother Geoffrey and their mother and father.

12. 152 Squadron, September–December 1940.

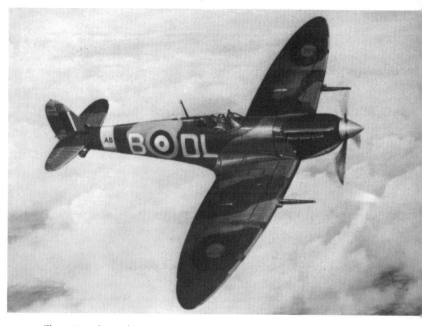

13. Illustration of one of Roger's later Spitfires, AB248.

Top and right:
14 & 15. Roger
and his Defiant
night fighter at
RAF Kirton in
Lindsey.
Below: 16.
Roger in
1999 looking
skywards at
a Spitfire and
Hurricane fly-
past.

17, 18, 19 & 20. *Opposite top*: Coastal towns, convoys, aerodromes attacked at the beginning of the Battle of Britain, period illustration. *Opposite page bottom*: A typical ops room at a fighter station, period illustration. *Top*: Men of the Observer Corps on the look out for enemy aircraft. *Right*: A period illustration showing the organisation of Fighter Command.

OBSERVER POST

BALLOON BARRAGE

FIGHTER AIRFIELDS. A.A.

H.Q. FIGHTER COMMAND

GROUP CONTROL

SECTOR CONTROL

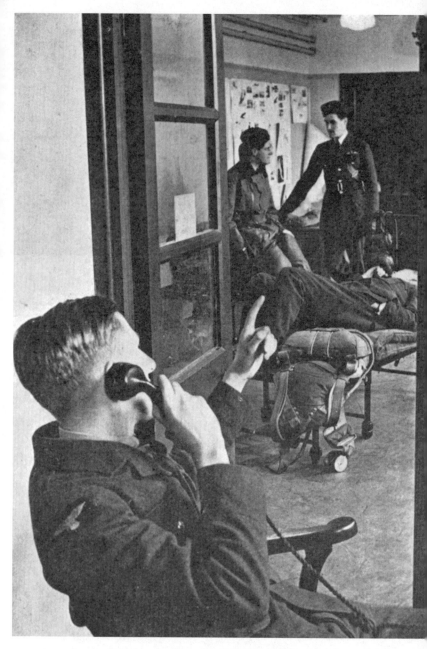

21. A squadron receiving the call to 'scramble' to intercept enemy aircraft from a fighter station.

22 & 23. Typical scenes in a dispersal hut of a fighter squadron. Pilots wait for the call to action, summer 1940.

24, 25, 26 & 27. Spitfire and Hurricane fighter pilots 'on readiness' summer 1940.

Above & opposite: 28 & 29. Instrument panel of a Spitfire from a 1940 manual.

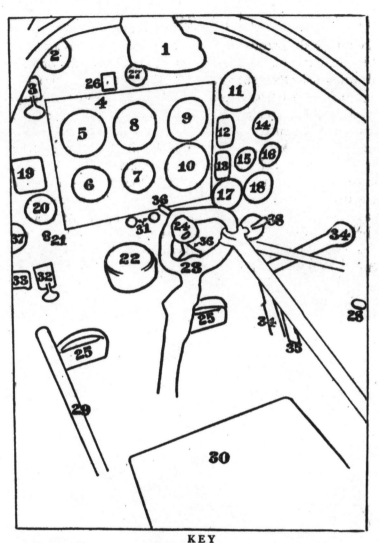

KEY

1. Platform for gunsight.
2. Flap position indicator.
3. Flap lever.
4. Instrument flying panel.
5. Air speed indicator.
6. Altimeter.
7. Direction indicator.
8. Artificial horizon.
9. Rate of climb indicator.
10. Turning indicator.
11. Revolution counter.
12 and 13. Oil and fuel pressure gauges.
14. Engine boost gauge.
15 and 16. Oil and radiator temperature gauges.

17 and 18. Fuel gauges.
19. Undercarriage position indicator.
20. Flying position.
21. Lights switch.
22. Compass.
23. Control column.
24. Gun button.
25. Foot stirrups in rudder bar.
26. Reflector sight light switch.
27. Dimming switch for reflector sight light.
28. Key for downward recognition lamp.
29. Radiator flap control.

30. Pilot's seat.
31. Floodlight switches.
32. Lever for lowering and raising landing light.
33. Throttle.
34. Pump for operating undercarriage.
35. Selector lever for undercarriage (to be placed in raise or lower position before 34 is operated).
36. Pneumatic brake lever.
37. Air pressure control for pneumatic system (guns and brake).
39. Fuel cock.

30, 31, 32 & 33. Spitfire pilots 'scramble' to intercept enemy aircraft, summer 1940.

This page & opposite, top: 34, 35 & 36. Spitfires in formation, summer 1940.

Above: 37. A Spitfire pilot shows how by pressing a red button on the control column 8 machine guns blaze into action.

Right: 38. Silhouettes of the Spitfire from a 1940s aircraft recognition manual, hugely popular at the time amongst the general population, and vital for fighter pilots to ensure they didn't shoot down fellow RAF aircraft.

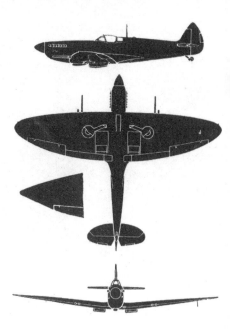

39 & 40. Hurricanes flying in formation during the Battle of Britain.

41, 42 & 43. Silhouettes from a 1940s aircraft recognition manual of German aircraft, from left to right, Messerschmitt 109, Messerschmitt 110 and a Junkers 88.

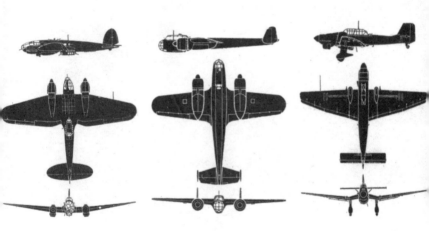

44, 45 & 46. German aircraft, from left to right, Heinkel 111, Dornier 17 and Junkers 87 'Stuka'.

47, 48, 49 & 50. German aircraft over England, *opposite top*, Dornier 17. *Middle*, Junkers 87s. *Bottom*, a Spitfire shoots great lumps off a Heinkel 111, remarkable film taken from an automatic gun camera fitted on the fighter, 1940. *Above*, another Dornier is shot down over London.

51. Vapour trails in the skies above London 6 September 1940, marking the dogfights of the Battle of Britain.

52, 53, 54 & 55. Spitfires returning to base, summer 1940.

56, 57 & 58. Spitfire pilots return from a sortie. *Above right*, a pilot reports to the squadron intelligence officer his tally of 'kills'.

59 & 60. The spoils. A downed Messerschmitt 109 (above) Messerschmitt 110 (below) both shot down during the Battle of Britain.

61. A 1940 illustration showing how the RAF checks the number of enemy aircraft destroyed. Historians have since analysed the combat figures and concluded that the RAF over counted significantly the number of enemy aircraft shot down during the battle.

AFTER AN ACTION A FIGHTER PILOT FIRST LANDS AND REPORTS RESULTS TO THE THE LOCAL INTELLIGENCE OFFICER WHO SENDS IN A PRELIMINARY ACCOUNT. AN ENTHUSIASTIC PILOT MAY MAKE SIGNALS OF VICTORY AFTER LANDING, BUT NEVER STUNTS OVER AERODROMES AS HIS PLANE MAY BE DAMAGED UNKNOWN TO HIM

...TER AN ENGAGEMENT ...RE ARE A GREAT PERCENTAGE ...DAMAGED ENEMY PLANES WHICH GET AWAY ...NE OF THESE ARE COUNTED AS A SCORE.

AT THE END OF THE DAY THE PILOT PROCEEDS TO HIS AERODROME WHERE THE OTHER FIGHTERS ASSEMBLE AND POW-WOW WITH THE SQUADRON-LEADER AND INTELLIGENCE OFFICER WHO WORK OUT DETAILED REPORT FOR GROUP H.Q.

FINALLY H.Q. FIGHTER COMMAND RECEIVES THE REPORTS FROM THE VARIOUS GROUPS, WHICH ARE CAREFULLY CHECKED AND VERIFIED WITH THE MESSAGES FROM THE ADMIRALTY AND WAR OFFICE, EVENTUALLY COMPILING THE DAYS TOTAL BAG. A LENGTHY AND LABORIOUS TASK.

BRYAN DE GRINEAU 1940

62, 63, 64, 65 & 66. More downed Luftwaffe aircraft shot down during the Battle of Britain. Such images (distributed by the Air Ministry in large numbers) was a welcome antidote for a nation facing the horrors of the Blitz. In the final photography the German crew is lead away from the burning wreck of their Heinkel 111 bomber.

After lunch I went down to dispersal whilst the rest of the Flight came up to the mess for theirs. 'A' Flight had now taken over in readiness and were all lying on the beds, some sleeping, some reading and the rest doing nothing in particular. The CO Peter, was there and was going to lead 'A' Flight or the Squadron if it were scrambled. Bottle was standing down this afternoon. He flew more than Peter for he had no administrative work to speak of in addition to his flying. Peter on the other hand had a constant amount of paper work to get through each day, although this was cut to a minimum for obvious reasons.

Only half an hour after I had gone down to dispersal the telephone rang and the orderly answering it called to the CO 'Operations want the whole squadron to immediate readiness, sir.' 'OK' Peter replied. 'Ring the messes and get the remainder of 'B' Flight down immediately.' This so frequently happened. For meal times one Flight was usually released to the mess whilst the other remained on readiness and very often the Flight which had just been released were greeted by a mess waiter to say that dispersal had rung through ordering them to return at once. It was a disheartening sort of thing to happen.

After the remainder of 'B' Flight arrived, I was allocated the position of Yellow two, to fly behind Chumley this time. Cocky was leading 'A' Flight, Dimmy was Green one and Sergeant Barlow was behind him as Green two. Ferdie was flying Blue two behind Cocky. The sky was quite clear again and there was a little wind coming from the sea to the south. Ops rang through to tell us to stand by for a possible scramble 'any minute now.' They had got a large enemy plot on the board forming up over Cherbourg. How I hated this tension. It was almost worse to be told to stand by than to be scrambled straight away without further ado. It was like standing poised on the edge of a swimming bath waiting for the starter to say 'Go', having already said 'On your marks – get set.' You couldn't even pull a cigarette for fear you wouldn't be able to put the case back in your tunic before you had to run to your aircraft.

Eventually the scramble order came and, as most of us had expected, we were scrambled to Southampton angels three-zero. We took off in two separate Flights and joined up as a complete squadron in a large 'V', for some reason best known to the CO. When we got to ten thousand feet the CO ordered us to get back into Flight formation and resume our battle positions. I think he was making us practise which was probably a good thing.

'Hallo Maida leader – Mandrake calling – Are you receiving me? – Mandrake to Maida leader, over,' came the controller's rather affected voice, which always irritated me. 'Hallo Mandrake – Maida leader answering – receiving you loud and clear – Maida leader to Mandrake, over.' the CO replied.

No further conversation followed until we were at twenty thousand feet, when the CO called up to ask control if there was any further information. Control replied that the bandits were still in the Cherbourg area but that we were to proceed to the aforesaid destination which today was coded 'Dustbin' of all names! The weather and visibility were perfect. We should be able to see Cherbourg at angels three-zero. I started looking in that direction but saw nothing except some more of our own fighters coming up from the east and north. There seemed to be nine or ten different squadrons milling about, some below us and some almost on the same level. Most of them were Hurricanes but there was one other Spitfire squadron besides ours. They gave me a sense of security I hadn't experienced before. We were certainly ready for the bandits this time if they came.

'Hallo Maida leader – Mandrake calling – what are your angels now? – over.' 'Hallo Mandrake – Maida leader answering – angels two-seven – repeat angels two-seven Maida leader over.'

We were now just starting to make vapour trails, and white plumes were streaming away from each of our machines, the vapour from Chumley's aircraft passing above the top of my head in thick opaque funnels. Vapour trails observed from the air seemed to give the aircraft and those flying them a sort of dignity, serene and splendid, which it is difficult to describe adequately. We reached angels three-zero and the CO called up control to advise them. They told us to orbit our position and to await further instructions. We began to circle and now, on the turn to the south, I could see more vapour trails out to sea and a good deal higher than our own coming towards us. The CO had seen them too. He called control, giving them the 'Tally ho', and told Maida squadron to start weaving behind and keep a good look out for those 109s above us. The vapour trails were coming from 109s all right. There could be no doubt of that. There were fifty of them at a rough guess and they seemed to be the advance guard for the bombers which, although I couldn't see them yet, must follow in a little while, but at a lower altitude. The Spitfire squadrons, having a higher ceiling than the Hurricanes, were always supposed to engage the fighter escort in preference to the bomber force, theoretically leaving the Hurricane boys unmolested to deal with the bombers. But so frequently the theory broke down in practice after the battle was joined and everyone, whether Spitfire or Hurricane, engaged what target they could.

The German bombers were now beginning to appear below us. They were at only about half our altitude and the Hurricane squadrons were waiting for them two thousand feet below us, orbiting their present position in perfect formation. I thought it was going to be thrilling to watch them pounce on the enemy and I hoped they would do so before we ourselves became engaged. There seemed to be just one large, compact block of bombers about a hundred strong, in much the same formation as they usually were, that is to say in ranks and rows stepped up from front to rear and flying close to each other. The whole body was now approaching rapidly and I was soon able to pick out the types of machines. They were a mixture of Dorniers and Heinkels but, oddly enough, no Junkers. 'Form Flights line astern – Maida squadron,' came the order from Peter. 'Tail-end Charlie – weave like hell.'

The rear man of each line was known as tail-end Charlie or, at times, by other and more descriptive words emphasising the fact that the position was both unenviable and at the rear.

We took up our positions and it was I who was tail-end Charlie of 'A' Flight. Our Flight was disposed as Red Section, then Yellow followed by White. 'Keep weaving Roger,' Chumley cried out to me to make certain I understood my job. I did so like a madman and had to use a lot more engine power than the rest of the Flight since I covered a greater distance than they did. The Hurricanes below us seemed poised ready to make their first attack on the bombers but I couldn't see them properly as I was fully occupied looking into the sun through the cracks between my fingers and at the vapour trails now directly above us, to detect the first sign from them that they had disappeared into the sun and were forming up ready to come at us, or else that they were losing altitude on to us. It was a constant vigil, permitting no respite or relaxation, and it was a considerable strain.

The ether was full of sounds from the transmitters of the various squadrons and from the ground controllers. I gathered from them that battle had been joined below us but I dared not look down for an instant. The 109s must soon come down on to us. Despite our altitude and the waning of the summer it was distinctly hot up here. I don't know whether it was the fact of my having turned my aircraft through an arc of 180 degrees about its longitudinal axis and, having done so, pulled it round in steep turns every half minute that made me think it was hot, but sweat was certainly pouring off my brow beneath my flying helmet down over my oxygen mask and dripping on to my Mae West and trousers. My shirt under my armpits was soaking too. The vapour trails above us had congregated in circles now which reminded me of a serpent about to strike. I felt convinced it was coming now and I had my right thumb in a hesitant attitude between the control column and the R/T transmitter not knowing quite which to concentrate on.

Looking into the sun through my fingers I could just make out the 109s starting to dive. Instinctively my right hand left the control column and operated the transmitter as I shouted 'Look out Maida aircraft – 109s coming down now at six o'clock above.' I switched over to 'receive' again and Cocky at once led 'A' Flight into a tight turn to port. I stopped weaving, to slide up close behind Chumley and follow. We practically formed a little circle, so tight was the turn, and I could almost feel the nose of Cocky's machine coming up behind my tail and felt a lot more secure because of it. The 109s had certainly picked us out for special treatment for about eight or nine of them flashed down into the middle of our circle, going straight through it and firing like blue murder as they passed.

I wondered if anybody had been hit. I certainly hadn't been. Cocky was down after them in a flash followed by his number two, to be followed by White section and then us, over on our backs, stick hard back and vertically down. 'Squareheaded bastards!' I heard somebody yell over the R/T as we followed in line astern of the German fighters. 'Keep a look out behind, Roger!' Cocky warned me. I was fully aware of the likelihood that the last of the 109s would probably be following us and that this first little escapade might have been a decoy to allow the ones still above us to come down behind us now we were going in a more or less straight line. If these were to be their tactics I couldn't help thinking that Cocky had been a bit rash or naive to have led us down so soon after the first lot and I found myself having certain doubts about him. But who was I to judge? We were committed now, and we could only wait and see what was going to be the result and make the best of whatever followed.

The 109s were going straight down and my airspeed indicator was resting against its extreme stop quite motionless. Occasionally I glanced in the mirror above my hood to see if there was anything on my tail but I didn't think much could catch up with us at this speed. How wrong I was. No sooner had the thought passed through my mind than white streaks began to overhaul my aircraft from behind. In a flash my right hand leapt to the transmitter and before I had pushed it forward I was shouting '109s behind us, 'A' Flight!' Then my hand found the control column again, pulling the aircraft away from the white spirals for a second and coming up closer behind Chumley in some illogical effort to find protection.

'Split up into sections, 'A' Flight, and shake 'em off!' Cocky called, taking his own section into a steep climbing turn to port. White detached themselves to starboard and Chumley led me into a very tight turn to port, but we didn't start climbing much although we had pulled out of our dive. We had lost considerable height during the last few seconds and were now down to the same level as the bombers and the battle. My altimeter was reading about seventeen thousand. There was nothing now on our tails and I called up Chumley to tell him so. 'OK, Roger, Keep weaving,' he said in answer to this and I pulled out a bit behind him.

Below us, but some way to the north, the main battle was in full swing and there seemed to be quite a few machines flying vertically with black smoke coming from them. Some parachutes were also floating down gently and some bombs had already been dropped, for Southampton, or parts of it, was pushing up smoke plumes and here and there I could see a sudden flash as explosives hit the ground.

'We'd better get into the bombers, Roger,' said Chumley as he pointed his aircraft in the general direction of the main invading body.

Suddenly I noticed black smoke coming away from Chumley's machine and I thought at first his engine was on fire. The smoke was sweeping past my own aircraft and instinctively I looked to see what was behind us, but there was nothing. 'Christ, I'm on fire!' was all that came from Chumley as he realised his predicament. He was apparently throttling his engine back, for I could see the blades of his prop slow down and finally stop altogether. I felt a sensation of horror for an instant, expecting to see Chumley's machine burst into flames at any moment, and drew back some distance behind him. I seemed unable to say anything to him on the R/T thinking that nothing I could say would be of any use.

Chumley pulled his aircraft round in a shallow turn to starboard, slowing down considerably as he went, his propeller quite still. I expected to see him bale out and hoped he would. The smoke seemed to get a little less severe, so his engine must be cooling off. 'I'm going to make for Tangmere, Roger,' I heard him say and saw him dive his machine out of the turn and in the direction of Tangmere, which was some way to the east of Southampton Water. 'Are you OK?' I replied. 'Oil pipe's gone for a Burton,' he told me. I said I would stick around until he got down lower and he said, 'OK I'll be all right, I think.'

When we had got down to five thousand feet the smoke from Chumley's machine had all but stopped and he was now above the aerodrome at Tangmere, manoeuvring into a position for a forced landing. I stayed at five thousand and watched him land, which he did with wheels down, and get out of the aircraft. From where I was I could see a lot of smoke coming from the forward part of the aircraft now it had come to rest, but the crash tenders and fire engines were already on the scene and were spraying foam all over it. I started to climb up again towards the north-west to see if I could find the others and offered a silent prayer of thanks for Chumley's escape as I went. I felt a bit shaken but I seemed to be getting inured to this sort of thing and felt fairly well blooded. When I had reached fifteen thousand feet again I checked my fuel, flew back to base and landed. I did not feel like talking, and went to bed; but I was restless and sleep came slowly upon me.

*　　*　　*　　*　　*

It seemed only a few minutes since we had first been attacked by the 109s and I had still to fire at something. The bombers had turned south or, should I say, the main body of them had. Quite a number had been shot down by the looks of it and the Hurricanes continued to press the rest. I was going towards them weaving violently as I went when I saw something that was to change my whole outlook. There was a Hurricane approaching the bombers from the port rear by itself and firing at one of them. The rear gunner was replying with what must have been very accurate fire for very suddenly the Hurricane became a mass of flames and the blow could only have been inflicted by the gunner, for there were no enemy fighters in the immediate vicinity.

I watched the Hurricane turn over on its back and fall away. The pilot himself was on fire as he fell from the machine. As the Hurricane went into a shallow dive, he released his parachute but, as it opened, its shrouds caught fire. The pilot, who had now succeeded in extinguishing the flames on himself, was desperately trying to climb up the shroud lines before they burnt through. I witnessed this scene with an hypnotic sort of detachment, not feeling myself able to leave it as I circled above. I was thankful to see the flames go out and the parachute behave in a normal manner. I felt a great surge of relief well up inside me, but it was to prove short-lived.

Two 109s appeared below me coming from the north and travelling very fast towards the south as though they were intent upon getting home safely to France. I disregarded the pilot hanging from the parachute and diverted my attention to the 109s, which appeared to be climbing slowly. I felt I should get my first confirmed aircraft now and turned on my back to dive on them. When I was in the dive I laid my sights well in front of the forward 109 with lots of deflection, for I was coming down upon them vertically. The leading 109 was firing and I looked to see what he was firing at but could see no other aircraft near him. Then I saw it all in a fraction of a second, but a fraction that seemed an eternity.

He was firing at the pilot at the end of the parachute and he couldn't possibly miss.

I saw the tracers and the cannon shells pierce the centre of his body, which folded before the impact like a jack-knife closing, like a blade of grass which bends towards the blade of the advancing scythe. I was too far away to interfere and now was too late to be of any assistance. If to see red is usually a metaphorical expression, it became a reality to me at that moment, for the red I could see was that of the pilot's blood as it gushed from all the quarters of his body. I expected to see the lower part of his body fall away to reveal the entrails dangling in mid-air but by some miracle his body held together. His hands, but a second before clinging to the safety of the shroud lines, were now relaxed and hung limp at his sides. His whole body was limp also, like a man just hanged, the head resting across one shoulder, bloody, scarlet with blood, the hot, rich blood of youth which had traversed and coursed through his veins for perhaps not more than nineteen or twenty years. It had now completely covered and dyed red an English face which looked down on but no longer saw its native soil.

The 109s continued towards the south with me in hot pursuit. I was a different person now and murder was in my heart. Nothing possessed me now except a hatred born of the devil. My emotions, my strength and all that moved me resolved themselves into a single force that concentrated upon one object – the 109s now in front of me but going downwards in a shallow dive. They had seen me and were exploiting to the utmost the advantage of diving speed which they had over the Spitfire. I was nowhere near within range yet. I was almost in a vertical dive behind them and yet they were not getting any nearer. I throttled back and thrust my emergency boost forward after it. The engine vibrated horribly and the black smoke belched and poured back from the exhaust ports. I was past caring for any consequences of this. I felt no fear at all. If the wings had fallen off my machine it would have caused me no alarm. It is surprising what one can feel if the right kind of provocation is provided. I knew now why men won the posthumous VC. I was an irrational being, totally unreasoning. I could see nothing about me, I was as though drunk, blind drunk, in that blinkers were cast to the sides of my eyes and only the direct forward view – the view of the 109s – had any meaning to me. I was engulfed, overpowered, encompassed by blind hate and anger which had to be consummated, satiated and was ravenous for retribution.

The 109s were getting closer and so was the sea of the Solent, eight thousand feet below. I settled the dot of my gunsight on to the rear 109 although it was far out of range still, and fired a desultory burst at the same time, giving the control column a slight fore and aft waggle which was as much as I could hope to do at this speed. I didn't expect to score a hit at this range and I don't think for a moment that I did, but it seemed to relieve my pent-up fury momentarily. I tried to visualise the face of the German pilot in the leading machine and to wonder what strange flaw in his character could give rise to such an act as he had so recently committed. I imagined him sitting there, the features of his face impassive, immobile, insensitive to feeling or to chivalry.

Perhaps he sensed that nemesis was about to overtake him, otherwise he would not still be diving so recklessly, and perhaps he felt within him a remote sense of guilt. I didn't know. I didn't bother to wonder. We were now only four thousand feet from the water and he must start to pull out soon. He did. He began to pull out slowly at first, followed by his number two. I slipped away to the side for an instant, to wait for him to come up again and to flatten my own dive a bit. Slowly he approached a less vertical angle, very slowly, as if afraid of blacking out. He was getting very close to the water now, too close; his change of attitude towards the horizontal began to be more coarse but he was still heading towards the water. It was too late. The nose of his machine hit the surface of the sea with a terrific smash and ploughed into it, hurling a spume of water before it which ran along the surface as the aircraft, now below it, continued to move forward; a spume like that cast from the bows of a speedboat travelling flat out. Slowly the rising water lost its momentum with that of the submerged machine and it started to fall, cascading on to the surface again, and then the surface was white but unruffled once more.

The other 109, conscious of the fate of its leader and knowing the reason for that fate, was doing its best to avoid emulating it. But in trying to effect this the pilot pulled out of the dive with such coarseness and disregard of the elementary principles of aerodynamics that both wings of his machine came off, folding like cardboard and letting the fuselage hit the sea like a meteorite. In less than a minute, this aircraft and its pilot were also swallowed up by the waters.

I watched all this from above and was unable to stifle the inane laugh of a madman. I laughed, and tears welled up inside me and poured down my face into my oxygen mask. My body was trembling all over as I woke up in bed bathed in sweat. It was all a dream – the kind of dream that came whenever I went to bed sober. It was the product of the anxieties which beset us, and the rumours which were circulating.

The blanket of alcohol which normally accompanied our nocturnal slumber usually sufficed to suppress these nightmares, so we drank to remain sane.

*　　*　　*　　*　　*

The general run of instructions spewed forth from the telephone in the dispersal hut and from the telephone in the mess and from the earphones of our flying helmets all day and every day throughout September 1940, until one day we got a new and strange order which was not at all like the ones we were accustomed to.

It was four o'clock in the morning of September the fifteenth when I was awoken by my batman who entered my room somewhat out of breath. 'Squadron to readiness Sir – dispersal have just phoned through.'

'What, at this time of night?' I said. 'Yes, Sir,' he said leaving the room and assuring me that he would be back with a cup of tea in a second. It was still pitch dark outside as I got up and looked through the window. I dressed hurriedly and heard the others getting up along the corridor. I didn't bother to shave or do anything more than give my teeth a hasty scrub to take away the taste of the beer which I had been imbibing the night before in some pub in Dorchester with Cocky and Chumley. The batman brought my cup of tea and just before I left the room for the mess Ferdie thrust his head into the doorway and said 'Better take your revolver along Roger – invasion imminent.' This was the only time I had seen Ferdie with an expression of complete seriousness on his face. I made no reply but did as he suggested.

That was what it was all about then. Invasion, a word that had for so long been on the tips of so many tongues. I took Ferdie down in my car and approached the dispersal area with caution as it was so dark, my headlights weaving horizontal searchlights in and out of the silent standing Spitfires. I was not quite able to believe that at last this thing was actually going to come to pass – an invasion of England – a thing that hadn't happened for almost a thousand years. I thought of my parents at home and most especially of my father who was commanding the local Home Guard contingent. He would be in his element if it came to a showdown. But I couldn't help feeling anxious for my mother and for that matter all the mothers who had just to stand and wait for the worst – undefended – helpless.

The whole squadron was at readiness by four-thirty and 'Brains' was there to explain the meaning of our early arousal. 'Brains' was in constant touch with Group HQ by telephone and ensconced himself on a chair by the side of it. The atmosphere in the hut was tense at first, until Cocky and Bottle arrived, bringing comic relief. Cocky was quick to sense tension and always was able to produce a gesture, an act or a remark that turned any such atmosphere to one of ridicule. The arrival of Chumley, the last on the scene, completed the farce. Chumley came through the door of the hut still in his pyjamas, his RAF overcoat wrapped round him and his battered hat on his head but back to front. He looked like a German sailor. Under his arm he carried his underclothes and uniform. His opening remark – 'What the bloody hell goes on around here? – bastard batman pulling me out of bed in the middle of the night' was drowned by a burst of spontaneous laughter and applause. Cocky got up from his bed and pulled Chumley's hat off while Dimmy unwrapped his overcoat. The bundle of clothing fell to the ground leaving little Chumley standing in his pyjamas in the middle of the hut while the applause reached a crescendo. The CO who seemed equally amused made some unavailing effort to impress Chumley with the seriousness of the occasion by saying 'Come on your Lordship you're not at Eton now – if we get a scramble as we probably will – there's an invasion on you know – you'll bloody well have to take off in your pyjamas.' 'Yes Sir – I'll do just that' Chumley replied and started to dress. Cocky did his best to prevent him and the thought of Chumley running to his aircraft in his pyjamas kept us in fits of laughter until there was no longer any hope of its happening. Chumley was dressed and ready for battle.

With every passing minute the tension got less and when the light outside was day, and not just dawn, the prospects of the invasion seemed to recede and with it, all our pre-conceived notions of what such an event would demand from us. At seven o'clock 'B' Flight were released to the mess for a quick breakfast.

7

First Kill: October 1940

As September drew to a close it became noticeable that the German bombing offensive by day had started to decline; not suddenly, but gradually, until by mid-October it was evident that it had been checked, at least for the time being.

Whether this slowing down was forced upon the Germans by economic necessity or by the morale of the bomber crews was purely a matter for conjecture. As time went by the bomber forces became smaller than their fighter escorts and finally the orthodox daylight bomber disappeared altogether giving place to a fighter with a heavy bomb slung beneath it. Thus was born the fighter-bomber, at worst only of nuisance value from the military point of view.

The RAF planning and operations departments had evidently realised that the Luftwaffe was suffering a considerable setback and were intent upon exploiting this to the full by throwing in reserves where the breach was largest. Although there were precious few reserves of any sort in Fighter Command at this time, the desired effect was to some extent achieved by increasing and sometimes doubling the number of operational flights for what fighters there were. Thus, despite the decline in the general tempo of the battle, there was no corresponding respite for us – in fact, quite to the contrary. It was annoying in the extreme, for everyone was tired, and tempers became short.

The comparatively meagre bomber complement that came over with strong fighter escorts virtually relegated the bomber itself to a provocation that would get our fighters up into the sky and provide an opportunity for them to be shot out of it. Bombs were very often dropped at random once the fighters had become involved and eventually the fighter bombers dropped their bombs when they saw our fighters taking off to intercept them. Towards the end of October therefore, practically all operations were between fighters. The Germans had every advantage over us, for they could choose their time and altitude and were free from any encumbrances such as bomb loads and targets on which to drop them. However, they had limited endurance and range, although the latter was increased by the introduction of an auxiliary fuel tank slung under the fuselage in place of the bomb.

They also had an advantage in that we were never scrambled until they had almost reached the English coast, often at phenomenal heights. For some reason, best known to themselves, our controllers invariably used to vector us directly towards the position of the enemy fighters, with a total disregard for inferiority of altitude, thus giving us comparative impotence and extreme vulnerability. The result of this was that, more often than not, we emerged from heavy cumulus as black specks in the eyes of the German pilots flying above us, usually in the sun and many thousands of feet higher than we were. It was not surprising, therefore, that we were pounced upon just when it suited the Germans and our losses were nearly always more severe than theirs.

In this way we, in our squadron, suffered casualties at a rate that was, in proportion to the number of bombs dropped, far higher than it had been during the blitzkrieg of the previous two months. It seemed to be foolhardy and it did nothing to improve relations between our pilots and the ground controllers. We were always at a loss for height and when the German fighters, having bided their time and chosen the moment to pounce, had attacked us, they seldom stayed to mix it with us but invariably continued in their dive, rejoicing in the safety of their superior speed. All the fighting we were able to do was in a vertical attitude and at best this was unsatisfactory, ineffective and unnecessarily dangerous in view of what we were able to achieve and more especially in view of the numbers of our casualties, which were considerable. It was also tragic that some of our experienced veterans were lost like this. However, ours was not to reason why. One day, one of our leaders showed some initiative when scrambled after some German fighters thirty-five thousand feet over Southampton by going on the vector reciprocal to that given him by the controller, and gaining altitude in this manner. This meant that when we turned eventually on to the correct vector we had almost the same altitude as the Germans and curiously – to the controller no doubt but not to us – we shot down quite a lot of enemy aircraft without any loss to ourselves. On landing, the leader was asked to account for his departure from orders, but merely quoted his results, which seemed an adequate explanation. The next day he was posted from the unit.

With the coming of winter the weather presented a further hazard to the less experienced pilots and several were lost because of it. I myself had the nasty experience of getting out of control in cloud and nearly had to abandon my aircraft in consequence. We had been flying through a heavy bank of cumulus when our leader turned to starboard without much warning. I was flying on his immediate starboard and I had to pull violently away from him to avoid hitting him. In doing so, I let my aircraft go into a high speed stall and it started to spin. Not being conversant with the procedure for recovery from spins by using instruments only I had to try to recover by trial and error methods and these were quite unsatisfactory. When my altimeter showed only three thousand feet I slid open the cockpit hood and released my Sutton harness preparatory to baling out. The very act of opening the cockpit hood disturbed the airflow in such a way that the aircraft recovered from the spin of its own accord and so I closed the hood again and eventually came out of the cloud base upside down and feeling very shaken. Shortly after this episode I had my first serious crash or 'prang'.

It occurred one afternoon when we had been scrambled after some single bandit flying somewhere in the vicinity of Bristol. The weather conditions prevented us from finding it, but we searched fruitlessly for a long time and were finally ordered to return to base and pancake. I noticed that my engine was not running so well as it might have been but, as we were over land, I didn't think it was worth returning before recall. Halfway over the Somerset and Wiltshire countryside my engine finally conked out. I was below cloud base at a height of about fifteen hundred feet. In these circumstances, there was no alternative but to make a forced landing. I decided to put the machine down on the main road running between Salisbury and Andover. I put my wheels down and manoeuvred into a favourable approach position. I came down a straight line of the road which seemed to be clear of traffic but, at the last moment, two lorries hove in sight and I was compelled to divert to a small field. I side-slipped my aircraft violently and my port wing struck the ground, buckled and tore itself away, throwing the remainder of the plane on its starboard wing, which in turn came off together with the landing wheels. The fuselage slithered along the ground for about fifty yards until it stopped. The aircraft was a complete write-off, but the only injury I suffered was a grazed knee.

These things were commonplace in the RAF and sooner or later they happened to most pilots. I only quote this instance to show how matter of fact such events were.

By November the sky bore the unmistakable signs of winter. The clouds replaced the clear blue brilliance of the former months and most of them seemed pregnant with ice. It was icy inside the aircraft too, for when we entered cloud, ice built up on our machines, most noticeably on the windscreen with a suddenness that was startling. We felt as though we were gripped in some large, chilly hand. Icing of the control surfaces did not present any major problem, for we were seldom in the air long enough for this to happen. The aircraft were also seldom at the same altitude for any length of time, another factor that helped to prevent serious icing.

Temporarily the threat of invasion had been stemmed and Hitler would have to think again. During the lull that now followed I was able to indulge more readily in the doubtful benefits of introspection, a process which I tried hard to resist, for with it returned my old dangerous habit of morbid self-examination. No form of self-analysis can be of any value unless it is completely factual and it would be a travesty of the truth were I not to admit that my self-analysis revealed, among other shortcomings, an underlying element of fear. I admitted to myself that my survival to date was probably due to caution and lack of aggressiveness at times when such caution and restraint should have gone overboard. I compared the duration of other pilots' lives since they had been in my squadron with my own and tried to analyse the reasons why they had gone and I had not. Among other things, I learnt that courage was an expendable commodity. I didn't realise this until I saw one of our most experienced and audacious pilots, having shot down seven aircraft since August, crumple under the strain. He had just returned from a battle and he got out of his aircraft and cried like a baby, leaning up against a wing trying to support himself. I had heard of this sort of thing happening to people under fire for prolonged periods of time in the trenches during the Great War, but I had never believed it. Now I saw it in reality and I could understand that those who censure it or connect it with cowardice are those who have never had to undergo a similar strain.

To a large extent fear finds its origin in the imagination and the imagination so frequently becomes more vivid and fantastic under strain. We all had to surpress fear for obvious reasons, not least was the desire to appear without it and so retain our own self-respect, for having lost this we are on the way down. There was a condition beyond the realm of fatigue to which one flew not as an animate thing at all but as an automaton, unfeelingly and unknowingly, without skill or care.

Looking back, I think it must have been this period of self-analysis that prompted me to respond to a call for volunteers to transfer to night-fighters. By the end of the year the fighter-bombers had given way to the night bombers and pilots were being asked to volunteer to train as night-flyers in order to combat this new menace. I was scared stiff by the prospect of flying a fighter at night, but believing as I did that my fear had to be sought out for what it was worth and nailed, I decided to put the matter to the test.

It was in early December that I bade adieu to the squadron after a good pub crawl around our haunts. I left with real regret those who had been such staunch and amusing friends foe the last three months.

The aerodrome to which I had been posted was in my home county of Lincolnshire, and lay about thirty miles from my home as the aircraft flies. It was about ten miles north of the city of Lincoln itself. The countryside rond the airfield was flat and at the time I arrived was covered with snow. The squadron had been formed only a week before and, therefore, its entire complement was new, that is, they had all come from other squadrons or straight from OTU's. At all events we were new to each other. In the RAF, however, people had the habit of remaining strangers at the most an hour or so and at the least ten minutes, particularly if they met in the bar. On the same station there were two other squadrons one was a Spitfire outfit which had recently come north to tidy itself up after the Battle of Britain and the other was the first American Eagle squadron, No. 71 which was equipped with Hurricanes and engaged in an intensive training programme. Some of its members, who formed its nucleus, had come from British squadrons and had served in them during the Battle of Britain, but the Eagle squadron itself did not operate in the Battle of Britain, in fact it did not start to operate until well into 1941. The Spitfire squadron was 216 squadron and was engaged in local defence and convoy escort work along the east coast. Our own was 255 squadron.

During the next few days the entire personnel of the squadron arrived, and we started to sort ourselves out and began training. Our CO Smithy, gave us a brief lecture on what our work would entail. We would be given three months' training to acquire and perfect the art of night interception and night combat after which we should go south and start to operate against the German night bombers. We were to spend the first month learning to handle the Defiant during the daylight hours so that we should accustom ourselves to its flying characteristics. The Defiant was a much heavier machine than the Spitfire. In addition to its two seats it incorporated a power-operated gun-turret, mounting four guns with an all-round traverse.

We started to fly these machines the day following our arrival. The Lincolnshire countryside lay beneath a mantle of snow and the whole panorama gave the impression of something inexpressibly bleak and melancholy. It was something of a novelty to me to be able to pick out the landmarks I knew so well from the ground. I flew over my home cautiously for I was far from happy with this strange aircraft. It seemed heavy and cumbersome compared to the Spitfire which was so delightfully nimble and sensitive. Above us, as we flew, was a sky laden with snow clouds with their bases little more than four thousand feet high. In these conditions the aerodrome was difficult to find, for roads and other landmarks were all covered with snow. Lincoln Cathedral provided a good landmark, for it stood serenely on the top of a fairly high hill dominating the city. There were a lot of other RAF stations close to ours, mostly bomber stations, but all constructed to the same set pattern, and as they all presented from the air the same configuration of buildings it was easy to become confused. More than once, a pilot had started to make his landing approach to a bomber station, only to realise at the last moment that it was not his station after all.

I had been allotted a New Zealander, a sergeant pilot, as my gunner and he was the very essence of enthusiasm and lived for the moment when he could fire at a German bomber.

Towards the end of our first month we began to fly during the moonlit periods of the night, to accustom us to conditions under which we should eventually operate. We had scarcely accomplished this when the German night bomber began to penetrate the midlands and the north. They raided Hull and Sheffield and these two places were of direct concern to us for they were both in our immediate vicinity and came within our defence area. We were ordered to start operating by night at once.

The art of night flying demanded an unquestioning faith in the instruments of the control panel. Night flying was in fact almost wholly a matter of instrument flying, particularly during the critical moments of take-off and landing.

For the first month during which we operated against the night bomber we had little or no success. We were vectored into a rough position by our controllers who were using a more delicate and therefore more accurate type of radar interception than that which they had used during the daylight battles. Even this was inadequate, for it could only place us into a position somewhere in the vicinity of the enemy bomber, and on a really dark night it was possible to be within yards of a quarry and yet not see it. We were virtually pioneers of night fighting.

At half-past eight I was summoned to the telephone and ordered to report down to dispersal at once. I took my flying coat from its peg in the hall outside the ante-room and, carrying my hat, left the mess for my car which I had parked outside. I drove the odd mile or so down to the dispersal hangar at great speed, wondering what was afoot. The intelligence officer who was always on duty at dispersal while we were flying, told me that there was an enemy bomber stream crossing the line of the Humber at twelve thousand feet and that we were to take-off at once, and orbit a position at angels one-five above the mouth of the Humber. My gunner was at dispersal when I arrived. Sergeant Fitz, as I called him, was almost beside himself with zeal when he heard the news.

We hurried to our machine which stood silently among the others in the dispersal area, looking like something quite sinister in its matt-black night camouflage – something motionless and inanimate, covered here and there with small crystals of hoar-frost which reflected the light of the moon and gave the whole scene an appearance of frozen immobility. The engine was started and in place of fire and smoke from the exhausts, a blue glow settled at the ends of each of them. Small cinders of ignited carbon came past the fuselage of the aircraft and were swept on to the ground. I called up my gunner and said on the intercommunication system 'All set Fitz?' to which he came back with, 'All OK this end Sir.' I then called up control and said 'Hallo Carmen – Hallo Carmen – Cushion 18 calling Carmen – are you receiving me?' Control came back to say that they were, and that I was to take off immediately.

I opened the throttle of the heavy machine and at once it began to move. I steered it by the alternate application of the wheel brakes towards the 'Chance-light' which was situated at the take-off end of the flare-path. Having reached the Chance-light I stopped the machine to await the green light signal from the officer in charge of the flare-path, without whose permission no machine could take off. Back came the green light almost at once and I swung the aircraft round on to the flare-path. The flare-path was lit only by a row of gooseneck flares at intervals of some fifty yards or so along the whole length of the grass runway. I pulled the machine into a diagonal attitude across the centre of the takeoff runway and looked over my right shoulder to see that nothing was attempting to land. I then made a second cockpit check to assure myself that everything was in order and confirmed with Fitz that he was all right.

I swung the machine round to face the end of the runway and eased the throttle forward. When we were airborne we turned gently to port and started to climb. I called up control and said 'Hallo Carmen – Hallo Carmen – Cushion 18 now airborne – are you receiving me?' – 'Hallo Cushion 18

– Carmen answering – am receiving you loud and clear – proceed to angels one-five over 'Shrimps' – Carmen to Cushion 18 – over.' I acknowledged this reply and pointed the aircraft to the north-east and upwards. We started to climb at the rate of one thousand five hundred feet a minute which was quite a steep attitude for this type of machine.

The sky towards the east was beginning to fill up with small pieces of cumulus which drifted over towards the west. The moon and stars were brilliant above it. The air was calm, as it so often is at night, and everything seemed to be in order. Yet I felt anxious for the future as we increased our altitude towards 'Shrimps', which, according to the code card, was Hull.

I had an uneasy premonition that something was going to happen this night that was not going to be routine. All the evening I had been conscious of something that had made me feel unsettled and restless. I didn't know what it was, but I knew we were going to come back to the aerodrome with some quite new experience behind us. I recalled the words of a card that my mother had sent me shortly after Christmas which bore a reproduction of part of the King's speech to us during his Christmas broadcast that year.

'Go out into the darkness and put your hand into the hand of God, and that will be safer than a known way.' It seemed to me that this was particularly significant, and at once I felt an extraordinary composure and was completely at ease. When we had reached our altitude above the Humber I called up control to tell them so. 'Hallo Cushion 18 – control answering – your message received and understood orbit your position and keep a sharp lookout for bandits in your immediate vicinity – Carmen to Cushion 18 over,' came the reply from control. We proceeded to orbit our position. I slid open my cockpit hood to get a better view, at the same time calling up Fitz to tell him to keep a good lookout to the rear.

The night was beautiful. Below us the isolated pieces of cumulus had gathered themselves together into a large bank of cloud which was itself being piled up upon by more broken pieces coming in from the sea. The whole of it was lit up with a wonderful iridescence by the moon above us and, when I could afford to take my eyes off the sky in front, I could see the shadow of our machine flit quickly and silently across the backcloth of cloud like some ghostly bird.

We had been orbiting for almost half an hour without seeing a thing, when quite suddenly, I caught sight, from the corner of my eye, of a Heinkel III gliding silently and apparently furtively towards the coast and out to sea beneath us. In a fever of excitement I switched on the 'intercomm' and shouted to Fitz 'There it is Fitz – below us – see it?' and switched over to receive. Fitz said 'No haven't seen anything yet.' While I was speaking to him I put the aircraft into a steep dive towards the Heinkel, for I was afraid that I was going to lose sight of it in the darkness. I called up Carmen and gave them the tally-ho and they acknowledged my message and wished us the best of luck.

The Heinkel was apparently unaware of our existence as we approached it from above, for it continued on its course out to sea. We came down behind it and on its port side, but we were going much too fast and overshot it. We wanted to get in front of it and sit in close formation with it so that our guns could fire backwards into the cockpit. Having overshot the Heinkel I pulled out sharply to port into a steep turn trying to absorb some of our speed in doing so. We pulled round into a starboard turn after this and came into the bomber once more. I felt certain that we should have been seen by the bomber's crew by now but it still persisted on its original course, and as we came in underneath and in front of it, we got no fire from its guns. We were about eight miles out to sea when I gave Fitz the order to fire.

Our aircraft shuddered slightly as Fitz opened up on the bomber with the four turret guns pointing directly backwards and firing up at the bomber's cockpit from a range of little more than twenty yards. I looked over my shoulder as he fired and saw the great Heinkel sitting gracefully like a bird of prey above us as though quite stationary. I could see our bullets hitting the bomber's centre section from underneath and the shots were like small dancing sparks creeping forwards up to the cockpit of the enemy machine. The flashes from our own guns were a luminous purple in the moonlight and their reflections cast their light back on to the perspex of the gun turret.

For what seemed an age Fitz continued to pour his shots into the front part of the Heinkel without anything seeming to happen. Then suddenly but quite slowly the huge aircraft started to roll on to its starboard wing tip, like a fighter in slow motion; very gracefully, and in a lazy but dignified way. The roll persisted beyond the vertical and I pulled our own machine out of the way for fear that it might fall on to us. When the Heinkel had got just beyond the vertical it started to dive and pull away to starboard and away from us, but there was no sign of fire about it at all. I think we had managed to kill the pilot for our bullets had pierced the perspex of its cockpit. We followed the bomber into its dive and closed in to it for another attack as it went down. We came up on its port quarter and moved in on it from a distance of fifty yards or so but in a vertical attitude. We were both going down towards the sea now and at a considerable speed. Fitz opened up again at the bomber and I told him to aim at the engines. He did so and shortly after he had opened fire, the port engine of the bomber caught fire. I was wondering what the crew of the bomber were doing or whether they were all dead. Perhaps they had thought themselves quite safe once they had crossed the English coast on their way home, and had been pulling cigarettes out and lighting up when we attacked them. I'm certain their front-gunner was not at his post when we came in at them. The port engine of the bomber was now beginning to burn fiercely and the flames from it were lighting up the remainder of the machine, and making its black crosses conspicuous. Beneath us was the top of a low bank of cumulus and it looked as though the bomber were going into it. I told Fitz to give it another burst before it went into the cloud and we pulled in a bit closer, but as we did so a small explosion occurred somewhere in the region of its port engine nacelle and flame and pieces of incandescent metal flew towards us and threatened to hit us. I kept the Defiant a fair distance from the bomber after this and Fitz opened fire from where we were. The bomber was now lower and nearer to the cumulus. Fire was streaming from almost the entire machine and the light from it illuminated the moonlit cloudbank beneath it, turning it a dull orange colour and giving a fantastic and cruel sort of beauty to the whole scene. I was pondering this scene in a detached sort of way when without warning the whole vault of the night sky burst into light. There was a gargantuan explosion and the very firmament seemed to reverberate about us as the bomber disappeared and dissolved itself into a gigantic white-hot cloud of fire, which turned night into day. The stars in their courses became a dull red in the heavens and the cumulus beneath became a vivid white – a ghostly white, superb in its awesome beauty. The Defiant was hurled by some enormous shock wave out of its course, like a leaf in the wind. The engine stopped for an instant, and then caught again.

For a few helpless seconds I was unable to unfasten my gaze from the scene. The cloud of fire spewed forth incandescent pieces of material trailing spirals of darkened smoke behind them. It descended slowly towards the top of the cumulus and as it approached the cloud top glowed a burning yellow. Then the blackened body of the aircraft's fuselage with oily smoke coming from it, could be seen against the whiteness of the cloud as the remains of the machine disappeared into it. When it had passed through the top of the cloud, the cloud still retained its luminosity – a vivid orange, mingled with black – which gradually became less bright and finally dim, as the fiery remains of the Heinkel fell through it. When it had gone, the night about us seemed horribly dark, and for a moment I experienced a feeling of utter horror and loneliness and my hands were shaking and my knees trembling. I headed our machine for home and called up control as we went to tell them about our combat. We landed at base about ten minutes later, taxied into the dispersal area and got out of the machine. I was weak at the knees as I jumped to the ground but I slapped Fitz on the back and congratulated him on his shooting. We went into the dispersal hangar and gave our combat report to the intelligence officer who was there, eager and ready to take it. Ours had been the first machine shot down in the squadron's short history.

Eventually I was posted back to a day fighter squadron in Norfolk and I slipped into what could be described as a regular and somewhat monotonous routine. I was able to take a fair amount of leave and spent some part of it visiting Anne. But I was becoming painfully aware that the love we had felt for each other was growing tepid if not exactly cold and my meetings with her became fewer and further between.

Before long we were compelled to leave the comfort and comparative ease of Norfolk behind. The squadron was ordered to the South of England. Fighter sweeps and fighter-escorted bombing operations by daylight over Northern France and the Low countries had become the order of the day. We could no longer undertake these sweeps from as far north as Norfolk, leaving at first light and returning home at dusk. We had to be on the spot. In June we were posted to Manston in Kent.

Our mess was in a girls' school in Westgate-on-Sea and our 'spree town' was Margate. Manston was the nearest but one of all our airfields to the enemy. It was a huge airfield and because of its proximity to the Continent and its great size, it was used as an emergency landing ground by any aircraft, bomber or fighter, which had encountered difficulties over on the 'other side' or was for any reason forced to come down in a hurry.

Daylight operations across the channel increased steadily during June. The fighter sweeps declined in favour of escorted raids by the bombers upon industrial targets in France, Belgium and Holland. One morning we had to rendezvous over Folkestone at 10.00 hours at angels two-zero, and having reached the prearranged altitude we began to orbit our position to await the arrival of the remainder of the raid. The weather was perfect. Over the sea there was some considerable amount of heat haze which made visibility in the horizontal plane poor, but this didn't affect us for it extended to only about a thousand feet above the sea. There were no clouds in the entire sky. The sun was already high and it would inevitably prove a trial to us later on. Looking down on it, Folkestone seemed a tiny town like any other mass of buildings nestling on the English coastline. The white cliffs running towards Dover appeared as an escarpment or a piece of pavement which borders the road. The straits and the English Channel were placid and smooth like a piece of tinfoil, shimmering slightly in parts where the sun caught its reflection, but otherwise quite still. The coast of France from Cap Gris-Nez eastwards to Calais and beyond was as clear as though it were a map. To the west we could follow it down as far as Le Havre where it began to fuse into the horizon.

The rest of the fighter escort had arrived. Ourselves and two other squadrons comprised the escort cover. Above us, the Biggin Hill wing provided the high escort at angels three-zero. Our own wing was now at twenty-three thousand feet and in between the other two. Beneath us the close escort consisting of one wing was awaiting the arrival of the bombers.

At ten o'clock the formation of Blenheims – sixty strong – arrived from the north flying, as always, in perfect close formation. Their top camouflage was excellent and had we not been looking for them we might never have seen them at all. The Blenheims were closely packed and were disposed in six lines of ten, stepped up towards the front, unlike German formations of the previous year. The close escort fell into position about the bombers, one squadron on either side and one a little below and behind them.

The bomber formation set course for France at once steering in the direction of Le Touquet. We followed above them. The Channel looked only a yard wide but it took us ten minutes to cross it. The bombers were in front of us and when they approached the French coast the flak started to burst at once. The bombers kept straight on; two were hit by the flak and one appeared to rear up on to its tail in the middle of the formation, standing there as though all the laws of gravity had been overcome. The other one spun away towards the ground in flames. The bomber which had been standing on its tail turned over on to its nose and its tail unit came off. Two parachutes came away and their occupants fell towards the sandy beaches of Northern France.

The close escort started to weave about the bombers and when we were above the coast the flak came up to greet us, bursting close by. We started to weave violently as though in protest at its accuracy. We crossed the coastal flak belt and the firing stopped. Black bursts lingered in the sky behind us and drifted slowly away dispersing themselves into the atmosphere. The bombers had altered course towards the east by the time I saw them again. Now the R/T natter started in earnest and every part of it included some sinister reference to the inevitable 109s. 'Hallo Sheldrake leader' called some voice back in England, we have a plot for you to the south of target – very many bandits at angels three-zero – Skittle-Alley to Sheldrake leader – over.' Control, wherever they were, had warned us. Sheldrake leader, whoever he was, replied that the message had been received and understood. I sat tense in my cockpit, all my reactions taut like the strings of a violin. There seemed to be a central agency in the pit of my stomach from which lead-lines emanated to control surfaces of my aircraft. There was no delay between my thinking and the movements of my aircraft. The bombers were beginning to make their run into the target and seemed motionless in their steadiness. '109s coming down at twelve o'clock – Sheldrake aircraft' somebody yelled. Sure enough there they were coming down in one long line from the south, from out of the sun, straight on to the Blenheims. They levelled out, about twenty of them, before they came within range of the bombers and spread themselves out into some sort of formation. The 109s started firing at the head of the bomber formation. White lines of tracer linked the fighters with the bombers. The bombers kept straight on not jinking, not wavering at all. The leading 109s turned over on their backs and went straight down to France with four Spitfires from the close escort racing after them. Two Blenheims broke away from the formation: one was on fire in its port engine and the other blew itself into eternity shortly after breaking away. There was only a cloud of oil-black smoke in the sky to mark the spot. '109s coming down on your escort cover,' a voice shouted. That meant us. Bubbles took the squadron round in a steep turn to port and we avoided the first attack from about ten 109s which had started to flatten out behind us but which now were trying to turn with us to port. We came round the full orbit and the 109s dived to earth without a shot being fired from us. The bombers had reached their target and the bombs were now falling on to it.

The bombers turned immediately to port and away towards the north. We kept on to the south for a minute or so to take up position behind them. Immediately the bombers had started turning away from the target area, I saw the bursts of the falling bombs on the ground. The whole earth seemed to shake to the rhythm of the shock-waves. There was a lot of fire from the ground and soon a lot of smoke covered the target. I wondered how many people had been killed during the last two minutes. The bombers were going faster now that their load had been unleashed. We had just turned round when 109s in force fell upon them. They came from every quarter it seemed. From underneath in groups of nine, from the port, from the starboard and from above in great strength. The close escort was overwhelmed. The gunners of the Blenheims were firing everything they had got at the attacking fighters and the whole scene about the bombers became a mass of fighting machines going in every direction imaginable. Five Blenheims had gone down from the formation and at least two of the Spitfires belonging to the close escort followed them in flames. 109s were going down too and parachutes hung in the air to the rear of the scene. As we approached, Bubbles called up and told us to spread out a bit and not to overcrowd. Four 109s were diving on to the bombers from their starboard top quarter and nine more of them were approaching from the opposite quarter. They were all going down in a straight line firing, one behind the other. The ones on the starboard started to flatten out as they got very near to the bombers and to pull up over them. The ones on the port were beginning to do the same thing and it looked as though someone were going to hit someone else.

And that is what happened. The four 109s from the starboard quarter started to climb when they had flattened out of their dive and the leading 109 from the other group went straight into the rear one of the first group. There wasn't much of an explosion, but what was two aircraft a second before, became simply pieces of them being flung far and wide about the sky with a terrific velocity. A parachute unfolded itself with nothing on the end of it and just seemed to stay there as though it would go on staying there for ever. When we reached the bombers there were no 109s in their immediate vicinity and we took up position round them, our squadron on its starboard flank and the other two on its port and above it. Four 109s approached from the port flank and from the same level as we were flying on. We turned very steeply towards them as they approached and opened fire almost on the turn. The 109s were firing as we met them. They gave us some desultry bursts but didn't hold their attack, breaking away downwards immediately. We had hit nothing. We turned the full circle and chased after the bombers again going full throttle to catch them up.

The flak had opened up again and once more the sky about us was black with it. Another Blenheim fell away from the formation and started to dive towards the Pas-de-Calais. Three 109s came from somewhere and sat on its tail. Six Spitfires from the squadron to the starboard of us dived on to them and the leading Spitfire shot the rear 109 down. It went straight into Calais harbour with a thunderous smash. The other two 109s were firing at the Blenheim, which was twisting and writhing like some wounded bird being cannibalised by a vulture.

The Spitfires were sitting on the tails of the two 109s and firing at them. They hit both of them. The engine of the rear one caught fire and fell away to the ground and the front one's port wing disintegrated under the hail of canon shells from the Spitfires, and it simply fell out of the sky in pieces. The Blenheim was by this time on fire and truly alight in both of its engines. One parachute fell away from it and its occupant appeared to be all right. The Blenheim fell into the back streets of Calais and there was a tall plume of black smoke and fire to mark the spot. We had just left the coast of France when three 109s in line astern came into our section, the two leaders firing but the rear one itself on fire. Behind the 109s were four Spitfires firing at them. They carried on downwards with the Spitfires on their tails. The rear 109, the one that was on fire, plummeted straight into the sea.

About three miles off the French coast we were attacked again by nine 109s who had been waiting for our return, sitting, presumably at some great height over the Channel. '109s at twelve o'clock coming down now' someone shouted as they came into us from the front starboard quarter. When they had finished their dive they were on the same level as we were and coming into us almost head-on at a phenomenal rate. Black and Yellow Sections on our right and nearest to the 109s pulled to starboard a bit to engage them and fired at them as they approached. The leading 109 was hit somewhere in the engine and flames started to come away from its nose. I think the pilot must also have been hit for the 109 continued to come straight at Black and Yellow Sections as though intent upon ramming into them. The leader, now a mass of flames, came straight into the section and hit Yellow two about his port wing with its starboard wing. It was a fantastic sight. Yellow two's wing came clear off and was thrown high into the air above. The remainder of the machine spun round like a catherine wheel in a horizontal plane at an incredible speed but seemed to lose no altitude at all. The 109 lost its starboard wing and, on fire, proceeded towards the sea like a rocket. Its other wing came off before it hit the sea. Yellow two, or the remains of it, spun more slowly until it in turn went into the water. The pilot never got out. After this incident we remained unmolested for the rest of our channel crossing. The white cliffs of Dover became something more than just a symbol of our ultimate safety when we were halfway across the straits. They appeared to embody all that had ever been written about them. They had been called, among other things, silent sentinels, bastions of freedom and white bulwarks. As we swept over them to the sanctuary of the Kentish fields beyond they seemed all that and much more. I found myself thinking of the unhappy land twenty-two miles to the south of us over which we had just passed.

Our first day at Manston was fairly typical of the remainder of them. On most days we did two sweeps. Sometimes we did three, but this was far from popular and we protested frequently. No notice was ever taken of such protests and the strain began to tell.

8

Biggin Hill

As the autumn approached I was finally accorded what I believed to be the ultimate honour in Fighter Command by being posted to Biggin Hill, almost exactly a year after I had first started operating with 152 Squadron in 1940. I felt a new person. I was posted as 'B' Flight-Commander in 72 Squadron.

The squadron had an Australian CO and my opposite number of the other Flight was a Scot who had been a policeman before the war.

The wing had a formation that was all their own and I had to spend my time accustoming myself to it for a day or two. They had perfected it through trial and error and its main peculiarity was in the 'cross-over turns' that were made in the air. If the squadron were flying in three lines abreast and the leader, in the centre, wanted to turn to port, the line on the leader's port would cross over the leader's line above him, whilst the one on the starboard went beneath him. The Biggin Hill wing invariably provided high cover. However, for a short while after my arrival there was a high wintery cloud base and we did not operate above twenty thousand feet.

I had not been there long when Anne sent me a letter, telling me she was getting married in a week's time and asking me to go to the wedding. She had already informed me that she had fallen in love with a doctor and I was glad for her sake that she had decided to marry him. I went to the wedding, as did my parents, and I returned to the station feeling very alone and rather sad. I also felt a sense of reckless insecurity that was in some way connected with her going.

A few days later near disaster came to me. I was getting out on what was my sixty-eighth sweep and leading Blue Section. We were giving top cover to a force of seventy bombers attacking the aerodrome at Abbeville. The sky was cloudless and our height was to be thirty-two thousand. At about twenty-six thousand Red leader (the CO), on my right disappeared for a second and then reappeared. I thought the sun was getting in my eyes at first, but then Red leader disappeared again and with him the rest of the squadron. When they came back they were flying a long way off on my right. I put my stick over to the right and found them coming towards me rapidly so I put the stick sharply to the left. They disappeared again and, with them, the remainder of the wing. I looked out of my aircraft and couldn't see anything much except a hazy blur of blue.

I looked in the mirror above the hood and saw my number two, followed by three and four, as though in a vertical dive and I wondered why they were diving. I heard my engine stop and felt the machine shudder. I couldn't lift my head. My knees and hands began to tremble violently and I passed out. The next thing I knew was that the ground was spinning up towards me and I felt terribly drowsy. I took automatic corrective action and, after two or three attempts, pulled the machine out of the spin. I wondered what had happened and felt perfectly all right. My altimeter reading was five thousand. I knew now what had happened and fumbled for my oxygen lead tube, finding that it had been torn from its socket. I had been starved of oxygen at a high altitude, a state of affairs that might easily have ended in death.

I returned to base and my oxygen apparatus was repaired but, two days later, the same thing happened over St Omer. I blacked out at twenty-eight thousand and came round at ten, spinning down on top of a forest. The day after this I almost dived straight into the harbour at Boulogne, coming round at three thousand feet in a terrific dive. The MO and CO sent me down to Farnborough next day with my oxygen mask and I was put in a decompression chamber. I put on my mask and an altitude of forty thousand feet was simulated, after which I passed out again. The MO was quick to diagnose the fault. He told me I had been damned lucky, because my mask just didn't fit properly. He supplied me with a new one and, after that, I was as fit as a flea at high altitudes.

Early in November we moved from Biggin Hill to Gravesend. We were billeted in Cobham Hall, the country seat of the Darnleys, and here we experienced the delights of really luxurious officers' quarters.

Then came a day of disaster for me. October had come and gone and the beginning of November had witnessed little that was in any way out of the ordinary. The squadron was operating smoothly.

In the middle of November the wing took off to escort a small force of Blenheims to bomb the German airfield at St Omer. We were at our allotted height and had crossed the French coast. There was not a cloud in the sky. We had some flak from the coastal belt but that was what we expected.

There was a lot of vapour in the sky and we were making plenty ourselves. Some of the vapour was above us and it was mostly in the direction of the sun. The sun was very bright and I couldn't see what was in it. We were to the south of St Omer airfield and the bombers were preparing to make their run in. Then, quite suddenly, from the corner of my eye, I saw two 109s in line astern coming up from underneath and over to my right. My section was flying well out to the port of the CO who was flying Red one, and Yellow Section was fairly widely disposed to his starboard. The 109s were coming up beneath Red Section and seemed to be flying quite slowly. I was feeling full of a most unnatural energy that urged me to give battle at once. They may be 'decoys', I heard myself saying. Perhaps they were, but decoys or no decoys they would be flaming wrecks in a minute if I knew anything about it. I turned my section over on their backs and came on to them, lining up my sights on the leader and allowing plenty of deflection. Decoys my foot! They were bloody fools and I was the master now.

I pressed the trigger and watched for the 109s to disintegrate. Nothing happened. There was no judder to the accompaniment of my cannon fire. No cordite trail left my wing edges. I gave the button a series of fierce jabs, but still nothing happened. I was in a panic and had to pull away from the 109s which continued up towards Red Section. 'Look out Red Section!' I yelled, and then the Luftwaffe came down on my own section.

I had fallen for the most elementary ruse imaginable and had involved my entire section in its consequences. Fifty 109s attacked us from all quarters at once, firing for all they were worth. I pressed my firing button again but still nothing happened. I turned the section into a downward spiral hoping to gain some speed.

Still the 109s came in at us and it wouldn't be long before we were all shot down. We had drawn the entire fighting force on to us. It didn't seem to matter. It was going to be a glorious end. I had always wondered what it would be like. I no longer felt any panic. I was composed and supremely cool and my body reacted to this. My reactions were faster than those of the enemy and I was pulling the section out of the way of the 109s by degrees with some supernatural skill that wasn't my own.

A 109 approached the port quarter of my machine firing blue murder and just seemed to stay there sitting at my cockpit door. I put my hand up to my face and buried my head inside the cockpit to await the inevitable. It didn't come, but my machine was hit in the fuselage behind me and shook under the impact. I looked out of the cockpit again and the 109 was diving fast towards the ground. My number two went down, too, hit in the glycol and trailing a long white stream of it behind him. Green one followed in flames and I supposed that his number two would follow shortly.

We were down to ten thousand feet and number two's machine was spinning, its airscrew still. The glycol leak had become more profuse and was swirling about the tail in spirals. There wasn't much time to decide what I should do. I could close my eyes and just sit there and wait. I closed my eyes and waited. There was still time to change my mind. I still had eight thousand feet to go. When I closed my eyes my mind became the receptacle for voices from outside.

I opened my eyes and pulled out of the dive, not looking back as number two hit the ground. I flew back to England, pondering upon the thoughts that had passed through my mind and feeling thoroughly ashamed of myself.

I shed some tears as I crossed the Channel, not only for the others but also in the inexpressible relief from tension. I felt as though I were on the brink of a nervous breakdown and recognised the symptoms of my previous one so well.

The armament people told me that there had been a faulty lead in the hydraulic gun-firing mechanism which accounted for the guns failing to fire. The CO and the station commander besought me not to worry about the episode when they saw me sitting disconsolate in the mess. The Group Captain took me aside and said, 'It wasn't your fault, Roger. It's just one of those things that happen every day. What are you having?' I liked the Group Captain. Everybody did. (He was killed shortly afterwards over Beachy Head, shot down in flames.) I said I would have a beer with him and felt a lot better. He was Group Captain Barwell.

The following day number two's parents came to the aerodrome wanting to know about their son. I was sent for by the station adjutant and introduced to them. They were both small people in obvious distress and I could see a resemblance to number two in both of them. They asked me what had happened and, after I had told them, they wanted to know if there was a chance that their son could have baled out and was perhaps a prisoner. I lied to them and said I hadn't actually seen him crash. This in fact was the literal truth, though it gave a false impression.

Why must they ask these questions? Why couldn't they leave me alone? Why couldn't I be allowed to forget? This was the price I had to pay. I was paying it now and I would continue to pay it as long as I – and others – allowed my mind to dwell on it. They asked me what sort of a pilot their son had been and I was glad they had done so, because I was longing for an excuse to talk about other things. I was the leader, I told them, and like so many leaders before and after, I relied upon my number two to give me cover and I had him shot off my tail. It was always the leaders who were the least vulnerable. It was always the leaders who opened the attack and got the Huns. It was always the leaders who got the medals, the *kudos* and the publicity, but they climbed to fame upon the corpses of their number twos and tail-end charlies. Now it had happened to me and I no longer wanted to be a leader.

At the beginning of December, after I had done my seventy-sixth sweep, the MO and CO told me that I was to go off ops for a rest and they sent me on a month's sick leave. After this was up, they arranged for me to enter the RAF hospital at Torquay for three or four months.

A lot of changes were taking place in the squadron at this time and the sweeps had been virtually suspended until the winter was over. A number of the others went to ground jobs of one sort or another or to OTUs. I said goodbye to those who were left, packed my bags and drove home. This seemed almost too good to be true and I was resolved to get fit and well and to throw off the impending breakdown that was creeping up on me. I thanked God for the heaven-sent respite.

9

Leave, Hospital & Recces

I spent my first week at home and found I was getting on my parents' nerves. I decided to push off on my own and go to the Isle of Mull in Scotland. This had been declared a prohibited district, so I had to obtain the permission of the Argyll police, which was duly granted. I also had to travel in uniform in accordance with the regulations. I had a sleeper from Euston to Oban, where I transferred to the little inter-island boat to take me to Mull.

It was exceedingly bleak and cold, but I think this was one of the reasons I had decided to come, for I knew in such conditions I should find the measure of solitude I craved at the moment.

There was a high wind blowing on shore when I disembarked and there was some snow on the high ground above Tobermory, a village which had become a training centre for light naval craft of the corvette and anti-submarine type. I had brought my shotgun with me, hoping I might be able to get some sport with the duck and wild geese that abounded in this area. I booked into the hotel overlooking the harbour and discovered it was almost entirely populated by naval officers' wives. I changed into civilian clothes and determined I would not set eyes upon my uniform again until the day I left.

My state of mind was such that I wanted to speak to no one at all. For the first week I deliberately avoided the other hotel guests and spent my entire time out of doors, walking about the island and allowing the high winds to blow all my memories and phobias away. After a time, the people in the hotel began to regard me as an object of curiosity. They seemed unable to become reconciled to the fact that I was a civilian, since there were stringent security measures in force to prevent people other than military and naval personnel with their families from visiting the island.

Moreover, their suspicions were so aroused by my frequent absences that I was obliged to convince them that I was not a spy. After this, they went out of their way to get me to become less unsociable and, to some extent, succeeded. Before long I was invited to a guest night aboard the Navy flagship and, putting my uniform on, I set out at seven in the evening in anticipation of what I was sure would be a marvellous party. It was a bit too marvellous. I am ashamed to say I got myself thoroughly and utterly plastered.

I slept like the proverbial baby on my return to the hotel and began to regret that, for some months, I had imposed upon myself an alcoholic ban. I began drinking again in moderation after this and felt a lot better. After three weeks I said goodbye to the people in the hotel and went back home, spending two days there before going down to hospital at Torquay. This was the luxurious Palace Hotel, which had been commandeered by the RAF for the duration.

There were about two hundred other officers in the hospital when I arrived, most of them aircrew recovering from some sort of prang or another. Some of them refused to speak or read, rebuffing all efforts on the part of the nursing staff to get them out of themselves. Indeed, they bore a very close resemblance to the unfortunates I had met at Netley and Beckenham. A great many of them were 'flak-happy', a colloquial term used to describe the condition, pilots whose nerves had been shot to pieces by continuous subjection to anti-aircraft fire. It was a gross misnomer, for there was nothing happy about them at all. They were quite pathetic and their cute rested within themselves, as no doubt they would find out eventually. There were other cases – burn cases, shock cases, surgical cases, and men wandering about with only one leg or, occasionally, no legs at all. Some had broken necks and their necks were held rigid in great plaster casts. Despite this there was little depressing about the atmosphere at the hospital. The staff saw to that. We were given very little time in which to sit about and mope for there was a strict routine, which included PT, swimming and tennis, to be adhered to throughout the day. They even went so far as to run a bus down to the town every evening for the traditional pub crawl!

I had to go and see the resident psychiatrist for periods of an hour every day. The psychiatrist was an eminent Harley Street man and I felt completely at ease with him. We discussed all manner of things and he asked me what I felt about the future. I told him I should be all right within a few months at the rate I was going and that when I left hospital I wanted to return to operations. He asked me why, and I told him that flying tired me, but that I regarded operational flying as the least fatiguing form of it. Poor man, he was completely bewildered by this. He said he would think about it and when, after three months, I saw him for my final interview he agreed to my request to be put in the fully operational flying category and I was posted back to Biggin Hill.

I had resolved during the last few weeks that I was going to make an application to join 91 squadron, which was on the strength of Biggin Hill but was stationed at one of the satellites at Hawkinge, outside Folkestone. I had heard a lot about 91 during my previous service at Biggin Hill and what I had heard appealed to me intensely. Its pilots flew individually and it very seldom flew as an entire squadron. When I told the Group Captain at Biggin Hill about all this, he readily agreed to a posting for me to 91, 'B' Flight, which was at the aerodrome at Lympne, a few miles to the south-west of Hawkinge.

I arrived at the aerodrome and went to see the flight commander, who was in the dispersal hut. He was a small New Zealander whose nickname was 'Spud'. I identified myself and he told me to go down to the mess and unpack. I asked him if there was any likelihood of my being required to fly that afternoon or evening and he said, 'No. Not today.' There was something in his tone of voice that made me begin to lose confidence in myself and, as I lay in bed that night, the same old fears started to well up in my brain.

The following day, when I came down to breakfast, I met the others in the dining room of the lovely house which was our mess, the residence of a former Air Minister, Sir Philip Sassoon. It was a truly magnificent place. Its gardens were designed and kept up in a lavish manner, and were a delight to wander about in after duty hours. The whole nestled on the side of an escarpment running from above Hythe Bay, along the north of the Romney marshes to the old town of Rye. From the windows of the house you could see the French coast when the weather was clear.

The pilots themselves were as heterogeneous a lot that you could hope to find in so confined a space. They comprised natives of almost every European country except Germany and Italy. This was no accident either. It had a direct bearing on the work of the squadron, which was primarily of a reconnaissance nature.

The reconnaissance we had to do was mostly along the coast and over the inland territories of occupied France, Belgium and Holland. For this reason the pilots were predominantly foreign and were selected for their knowledge of the areas over which we flew. Naturally, the majority of them were French – in fact, the CO himself was French when I joined the squadron. There were Dutch and Belgian pilots, one or two Americans, Czechs, Poles and

Norwegians. Apart from these there were those from the Dominions and last but not least, a few British. Rank was a thing to which little or no significance was attached. Apart from the CO himself, there were over half a dozen flight lieutenants in the squadron, of which I was one, but their duties were in no way different from those of the other pilots. The two flight commanders, of course, had the administrative authority consistent with their position, but even this involved little beyond the duties of those in the remainder of the squadron.

Primarily the reconnaissance work was concerned with shipping. Enemy or enemy-controlled shipping had a very high respect for the potency of the RAF in the close confines of the English Channel, and it was seldom that any ships left harbour during the hours of daylight. In the harbours, they relied for protection on the flak defences which were very considerable. When they had to move, they did so only in convoy and, if this were impracticable, they had a large escort of accompanying 'flak-ships' to ward off aerial attacks. Our reconnaissance areas ranged from Le Havre in the west to The Hague in the east. Between these two extremities lay the harbours of Fécamp, Dieppe, Le Tréport, the Somme Estuary, Boulogne, Calais, Gravelines, Dunkirk, Nieuport, Ostend, Zeebrugge, Blankenburg, Flushing, and the sandy beaches of Holland up to the Hague.

Any shipping passing up or down the Channel had to find sanctuary by daylight in one of these ports, otherwise they were spotted and attacked from the air unless the weather were so bad that this was impossible. Our job was to spot and report the ships in the harbours or outside them. If a ship or convoy were behind schedule in any way, we sometimes used to catch them in the open sea at dawn before they reached port or, if they seemed to be in a particular hurry to leave port in the evening, we used to catch them outside, forming up at dusk. The dawn and dusk reconnaissances were therefore the most likely ones on which to find shipping out of harbour. We had to report the facts at once to the IO on return to base, and a strike of anti-shipping aircraft would be laid on immediately. Anti-shipping Hurricanes were disposed close at hand at Manston. We were not allowed to report our finds by radio for fear of alerting the enemy, unless the target were of such significance that it was worth the risk.

We were required to report upon the positions and the estimated tonnage of ships in harbour and Intelligence were able to deduce from these reports specific knowledge regarding the ships, which was entirely their province and which, no doubt, was of some value to them. We hoped so. This was, then, our primary function as a squadron. All reconnaissance work was carried out by an aircraft flying alone. Unless otherwise instructed by Intelligence, a reconnaissance would go from Dieppe to Cap Gris Nez on the westward run and from Ostend to Cap Gris Nez on the eastward run. This was the stereotyped 'recce' and one pilot would do one run whilst another did the other. They were known as the 'bus routes' and were covered at dawn and dusk as a matter of routine. In between these times, if Intelligence required other 'recces', they would have to ask for them. Often they did.

In addition to watching shipping we had also to furnish a fairly comprehensive weather report for these areas or any other area that Group Intelligence might designate. They used sometimes to ask for a weather report for the Lille area, for instance, with a view to a possible daylight raid, and emphasis was laid upon the extent of cloud in that area, and the suitability or otherwise of the weather conditions. It was an interesting job and one that was not without its responsibilities or repercussions. The manner in which a reconnaissance was carried out was the sole concern of the pilot and each pilot devised his own methods dependent on time of day, weather conditions, probability of enemy interception, extent of flak, and his own personal likes or dislikes. It was significant that no two pilots seemed ever to undertake a 'recce' in the same way. Some flew high and others at 'nought' feet. Some approached the area in question from the sea and returned along the enemy coast to base, whilst others would cover the area in the reverse direction. Some hugged the cloud base and others would brazenly ignore it and, in this way, the enemy was never certain where or when the routine 'recces' would come. Our casualties were therefore surprisingly light. It was our primary duty to report, and we were discouraged from engaging the enemy. We were expected to fight our way out if necessary, but to avoid interception or commitment to battle if possible.

Reconnaissance work was arranged entirely among ourselves and no one was ever compelled to undertake it. Those who disliked 'recce' work were usually employed upon the next of our jobs, which was Air-Sea Rescue spotting and patrol escort. Last of our duties was the ordinary dawn and dusk patrolling, undertaken as a matter of course. The patrol area extended from the North Foreland to Brighton or Hastings.

Our CO was Squadron Leader Demozay – 'Moses' as he was affectionately called by most of us. He was French and came from Paris. He was about thirty and at the beginning of the war was a non-flying liaison officer between the French 'Armee de l'air' and the RAF squadrons in France. When the blitzkrieg hit France in the spring of 1940, Moses, with only a few hours' flying experience, clambered aboard an RAF Harrow transport and started it up. He told a lot of ground personnel to come aboard and, discovering they were mostly Geordies, flew them to their own part of the world, landing them intact at Acklington, near Durham. In 1940 he undertook a course at OTU and became a fully qualified fighter pilot, afterwards collecting the DSO and bar, DFC and bar, his own country's Croix de Lorraine and the Croix de Guerre with nine palms. He had shot down over twenty German aircraft, mostly when based at Hawkinge and Lympne. He was very temperamental and distinctly unorthodox as a pilot, but in no way did this trait detract from his efficiency.

'Spud', my flight commander, was small, unimposing in appearance, and almost bald. His unassuming air concealed a wealth of humour and a strong personality from those who were strangers to him. He had flown behind 'Sailor' Malan, the top-scoring fighter pilot in the Battle of Britain and his record and prowess in the air were impressive. Despite this, Spud had no 'gongs' and it was not difficult to understand why. He had no time for senior ranks and was unusually undiplomatic towards them. However, he did eventually get his decoration not long after I met him.

In our Flight there was 'Heapo', an Englishman. He and Billy were the youngest in the whole outfit, being just twenty and nineteen respectively. They were great friends and they were both as wild on the ground as they were reckless in the air. Billy's speciality was shooting up gasholders and flak towers over on the other side, whilst Heapo used to strafe ships that he and only he seemed to find among the Dutch islands. His ships always sank and Billy's gasholders invariably exploded or caught fire.

There were two other Frenchmen in 'B' Flight. Jean Marador was small, dark and swarthy, and was always recognisable in the air because of his ebullient, almost aerobatic flying. He came from the Gironde and his compatriot, Demolines or 'Demo', who was very young, came from Lyons. Demo was inclined to belittle himself and seemed to consider it a great privilege to be in the squadron. But if there were no flying he was miserable.

The pilot I knew best, the one I liked the most and spent the best part of my time with, was 'Scottie', a flight-sergeant and a New Zealander. I seemed to know him the moment I met him, as though I had encountered him in some previous existence. When we did dawn or dusk patrol with two aircraft, he used to arrange it so that we did it together and the same thing applied when we were engaged in air-sea rescue escort. He always came with me in my car and, as he hadn't learnt how to drive, I taught him.

He was twenty-two and much the same sort of build as I was. He was always cheerful and laughed a lot. He hadn't had a great deal of confidence in himself since his first trip, when he did just about the most stupid thing possible and dived through the flak barrier at Boulogne to strafe a U-Boat lying in dock there. He never tired of recounting this story and admitting how bloody stupid it had been.

At six o'clock one evening Jean and I went up to dispersal and on arrival Jean took up the phone and requested from operations permission to take a new pilot – me – on a general sector recce.

Operations approved and Jean said that we would take off at ten past six. We took off and I slid up beside Jean on his port quarter and about five yards from him as we left the English coast above Folkestone and headed out towards Cap Gris-Nez. The sky was clear except for a few bits of broken cumulus at ten thousand feet or so over the sea. Visibility was perfect and we climbed up to about five thousand feet halfway between the English and French coasts. The sun was sinking and its light was not brilliant as it shone out from behind the cumulus.

The high promentary of Cap Gris-Nez, sloping gradually on either side to Boulogne and Calais, came into view a few minutes after we had left the English coast, and we held our course towards it. When we were about two miles off the coast the flak started to come up at us and burst uncomfortably close to our aircraft. Jean went into a fairly steep dive but maintained our previous course. I followed, keeping about fifty yards to his port and we crossed the French coast at two thousand feet and at a speed of about four hundred miles an hour above Wimereux.

Once over this coastal belt we continued on our course to the south and the flak ceased altogether. We came down to almost zero altitude, or what was more commonly known as 'nought' feet, above the French countryside and Jean called me up and told me to get into line astern. I did so and kept a little to one side to escape the turbulence from his slipstream. The Pas-de-Calais area seemed flat and deserted from our vantage point and, apart from a few isolated farmsteads and villages, there seemed to be few signs of targets which we could profitably expend our ammunition upon. Jean kept his speed within the three hundred mark all the time and we started to make a shallow turn to port, somewhere north of Hazebrouck. There seemed to be very few people about on the ground. We turned almost due east and saw nothing that could possibly constitute a military target. There were some livestock grazing peacefully in open fields. They turned their heads upwards and inclined a bit as we passed directly over them and then went on chewing the cud, unperturbed. I could see a small village to our immediate front and noticed that Jean seemed deliberately to point the nose of his aircraft at it and hold it there. We were just above the height of the telegraph poles as we approached the village and I had to keep a constant lookout for them and other high obstructions. Jean's aircraft was now beginning to weave in and out of the high poplar trees which surrounded the village. The village stood on slightly higher ground than its immediate neighbourhood and I noticed this only when I discovered that my machine was suddenly below the level of the tops of the telegraph poles. I pulled it up abruptly to avoid them. Jean had turned into a steep bank to port and was on the other side of the village when I saw him next; he was coming round to meet me, having made a complete circuit of it. I thought that he was trying desperately to find something on which he could justify emptying his guns but there was nothing. I passed over the village, the centre of which was dominated by a church with a ridiculously high spire. Looking down on to the buildings, the only human being I could see was a small girl not much more than four years old sitting on the doorstep of a farmhouse. She looked up at me and ran into the house. It was a large farm with a yard almost completely covered by a dung heap and there was a tractor of some description lying alongside the wall of one of the buildings. I made a circuit of the village and then followed Jean out to the north-east. He started to climb and we got up to two thousand feet a few minutes after leaving the village. 'Doesn't seem to be a bloody thing about – we'll take a gander around the coast I think – probably find some Jerries there.' I said 'OK' and we set course towards the coast. Jean called out and said 'What's this below us? Looks like some Jerry bike battalion or something – keep closed up a bit and follow me down.'

Below us there was a party of about twenty-five people on bicycles riding in two rows on the right of the road going towards the Belgian frontier and appearing to conform to some distinctly military formation or pattern. I couldn't see for certain who they were from my position, but trusted that Jean knew what he was doing and meekly complied with his instructions. I switched my firing button on and adjusted my gunsight when he called up to say that he was going down on to them. We were about a thousand feet above the road when I saw him lose altitude towards the bicycle formation about a mile in front of us. I jinked out to starboard a little as his slipstream hit my machine, throttled back a little and pushed the stick forward. I saw Jean open fire and the two ranks of cyclists immediately became a disorderly mass of men and cycles which spread all over the road. I came down on to them and fired, not aiming consciously at anyone of them in particular but at the centre of the carnage.

They were Germans. I could see that by the unmistakeable shape of their tin helmets. Most of them were sprawled about the road, others ran off it, and over fields to the side. Some lay on their backs and looked up in to the sky, their faces covered with blood and a look of incredulity in their eyes as they watched my aircraft pass over them. Small things I noticed within the short space of time, but things which I should see again vividly in the months and years to come. One of the cyclists was still on the road and still on his bicycle and became impelled into the air as with the force of some invisible sledgehammer, my cannons hit him and launched him like a human rocket, his limbs seeming to clutch the air before he hit the dusty road surface, pushing it away until he stopped moving. One of them was facing sideways as I hit him and he reeled over his bicycle with a suddenness that was alarming, the cylindrical gas mask container slung diagonally across his back seeming to swing up around his neck and to throttle him. There was blood and horror on the road as I finished firing. Jean was some distance in front now and starting to turn steeply, coming round for another attack. I followed up into a turn to port over the sandhills and when I was round the scene on the road below was a complete shambles. One or two of the Germans had escaped our fire and were hurrying across the fields to the side. The road was stained by pools of blood which increased in size as we came down again.

I began to feel a horrible revulsion for what I was doing. However much I tried to hate the Germans, I ended by despising myself.

I came down again on to the target and before I pressed the gun-button I could see the faces of the wounded in the road and they seemed to cry out for mercy. I could not hear their cries but could sense what they thought and felt unnerved. I was in the grip of conflicting forces, one of which told me to exercise mercy and the other to finish the bastards off. Yet there was a third which prompted me to fire for fear of appearing squeamish to Jean. I compromised. I pulled the nose of the machine up to the horizon and pressed the gun-button allowing the shots to pass into space innocuously. Jean flew out to sea and I followed thankfully feeling very dissatisfied with myself. I had failed to make a decision, I should never have gone to war that day.

Throughout the spring and summer of 1942 the squadron continued to operate along and about the coastal belt of Northern Europe. Our radius of activity was increased and stretched and frequently we were called upon to go as far east as the Zuider Zee and as far west as Le Havre. On these occasions there was no room for error for we carried no auxiliary petrol tanks and our normal supply was only just sufficient. Those who felt inclined, foraged inland and attacked ground targets of different kinds, and ships at sea came within the fire zone of our machine guns and cannons.

We continued to spot for those unfortunates who were compelled to abandon or ditch their aircraft over the sea, and to direct the rescue boats towards them, hovering above them until they were safely back in harbour.

I was to learn, and latterly to perfect, or so I thought, the art of shooting up all manner of ground targets and seaborne traffic under the inspired leadership of those who had made such practices their métier, chiefly Billy and Heapo. This was an entirely new sort of war for me but after my initial squeamishness I took part in it with just as much ruthlessness and callous indifference as to targets as the others. It was the order of the day. But I grew to hate it.

Scottie and I used to pair up most of the time for spotting and patrol work as we seemed to understand each other in the air.

One night when the moon was brilliant we decided to go over to the other side and do some moonlight intruding and strafing work among the aerodromes and the rail and road traffic. Since there was a curfew imposed on civilians after a certain hour we were therefore fairly confident that any success that attended our efforts would certainly be at the expense of the military forces of the third Reich and not at those of the hapless civilian population.

The moon was high in the sky before midnight and although it wasn't full, it cast plenty of light on the world beneath it. It was after eleven when I met Scottie at the dispersal hut. He came in with a large bundle of maps under his arm and an intensely excited look in his eyes. Scottie took his cap off and threw the maps down on the table and said, 'What a night for a party.' We laid the maps out on the table and proceeded to study them closely, with special regard to the aerodromes and their adjacent landmarks.

Three of the mechanics came into the room from their tent next door and asked me when we were due to take off and I told them in about five minutes. We made our final arrangements and took off.

Scottie came up alongside me and we exchanged OK signals with our thumbs before settling down to climb across the channel. Folkestone disappeared beneath our wings, its only lights being those from the traffic signals which flickered from red to green in an absurdly inconsequential way. There must have been some rain falling recently for the roads and pavements were wet and gleamed in the moonlight.

Our own bombers were out. It was obvious they would be on a night like this, but there were other reasons for our knowing this. Along almost the entire coastline from Le Touquet to the west as far east as we could see, there were searchlights stabbing the sky and in some places bursting flak. The searchlights were arranged in groups, it seemed, and placed at fairly regular intervals along the coast. Some of them were just pointing vertically upwards and were quite stationary while others wavered about the sky, attached to some central light which occasionally doused itself. We crossed the coast somewhere between Calais and Gravelines. There was a little light flak but nothing to alarm us. We were lit up by the searchlights several times but it was not difficult to evade them by diving and altering course. We came down to about a thousand feet and streaked across the French countryside like nocturnal beasts of prey, like wolves bent upon getting some defenceless chicken. Beneath us there were rivers flanked by poplar trees, and the moon shimmered on the water and it looked beautiful.

We were flying over a road, and Scottie for the first time broke radio silence and shouted to me that there was a car turning out of a village and onto the road which we had just crossed. I looked in the direction that he had indicated and saw it. It seemed to be a large car. It looked the sort of car that might be used for transporting military personnel of high rank about the place. We didn't know but we needed to found out. I acknowledged Scottie's message and went down to have a look. It was a military vehicle all right, for it greeting us with a volley of fire from what appeared to be some sort of light automatic mounted at the back. I called up Scottie and told him to get into position to attack as I pulled round in front of the car to get myself lined up.

Scottie acknowledged, and started to come down. I waited to see what was going to happen. The car was still moving at a pretty high speed and the road was as straight as the French roads usually are. I was orbiting at an altitude of about five hundred feet and to one side of the car. Scottie came down slowly in a shallow dive to line himself up on the back of the car. The Germans saw him coming and opened up on him with their light automatic when he was far out of range. The car began to snake from one side of the road to the other and to slow down considerably.

Scottie's Spitfire came nearer and the moonlight played about the cockpit canopy and the top surfaces of his wings. Suddenly I saw the fire from the ports of his cannons and looked at the car on the road. It was snaking about even more violently than before and was getting slower and slower.

The cannon shells sliced through the car like a giant fret saw. It was still swerving when it happened, but that was its last swerve. It hit a tree on the left side of the road and the back of the car lifted from the road until the whole had lined itself up vertically against the tree, jettisoning its five occupants into the air.

I followed Scottie up. 'Wacco Scottie' I said, by way of congratulation. At five thousand feet I levelled out and started to turn to port. The coast of France was about twenty miles away to the north and beyond it the Channel gleamed like a silver ribbon, with the darker English land mass beyond it. Searchlights still pierced the sky like the antennae of some huge insect trying desperately to settle upon something and unable to find it.

We had been up for almost three quarters of an hour when I saw a train, or rather the white smoke from one, winding its way up towards the north across the flat plains. There was no time to go to St Omer now for we had already wasted too much time on the staff car. The train was a long way away from our position and appeared to be travelling pitifully slowly. I drew Scottie's attention to it. He acknowledged, saying that it would make a nice bonfire in a minute or so.

We lost altitude very quickly towards the train and by the time we were at a thousand feet we had overtaken it. It didn't seem to matter. It couldn't get away. It would be a sitting duck. It had no guns on it and it couldn't even jink from side to side as the staff car did. We went into it with the reckless enthusiasm of killers, the sort of mentality that we had acquired. We had no thought for the engine driver nor the unfortunate occupants of his train. I led the attack and placed my gunsight a little in front of the engine and on its left side. Scottie was some distance behind me. As I got down almost level with the train I noticed that it was really travelling quite fast. I could tell that by the angle of the smoke plume as it lay almost flat on the top of the engine cowling. The train was drawing seven carriages and two trucks; I counted them as I passed them on my way up to the engine before I pressed the trigger. My first cannon shells hit the front of the boiler and steam swept back from it along the body of the engine. I turned my fire, as best I could, back towards the driving cab. I gave a short sharp burst into the cab and saw one of the occupants throw himself out. I was past the train and called up Scottie to make his attack. Scottie came down in his own almost inimitable style, that is to say jinking first this way and then that, slipping a little height off to port and then to starboard, determined to place the dot of his gunsight firmly upon the target and keep it there for as long as possible. The bullets from Scottie's guns had now caught up with the rear coach and were piercing its roof. There was no spectacular explosion or anything of that sort. As the fire from Scottie's guns ran along the tops of the passenger wagons I got ready to expect anything. One door opened and then closed again as though whoever had opened it had thought better of it after all. Then the door opened again and I could see a limp figure hanging on to it and sliding off it on to the track to be lost from view in the long grass of the railway embankment. The door kept swinging to and fro and no one else left that compartment.

Scottie had by now broken off his attack and had started to gain altitude in a left-hand climbing turn. He called me up to say he had run out of cannon fire and suggested that I should finish the train off. Up to now there was little appreciable damage to the train.

My attack seemed OK. The engine filled my entire gunsight until my propellor almost hit it. The train exploded and became like a torch flashing through the now darkening night. Flames enveloped the entire body of the boiler and licked back as far as the rear of the second coach. But that wasn't all. The track, or the wheels, began to disintegrate and the train jumped the rails.

Curiously enough the train left the rails at a point which, from a destructive point of view, couldn't have been better. The train was coming to a bridge. It wasn't a high bridge but it was a bridge nevertheless and it carried the track across a road which at this point was banked on either side of the bridge. At the bottom of the embankment there were six round oil storage containers.

The train left the track just before it got to the bridge and ploughed through the brickwork of its sides. The engine hit the sloping embankment on the other side of the road with the impetus of its former speed and still trailing the first two carriages proceeded to make straight for the oil storage containers. We were watching from a thousand feet now and the light-flak from the defences started to come up at us.

I was watching a string of green tracers curving up towards Scottie's aircraft when the engine of the train hit the oil storage tanks and the last of the green tracers became detached from the ground and no more followed it. Those that remained in the air seemed to go out and the whole sky lit up. Scottie's plane looked like some frightful phantom against a sky that was suddenly bright yellow.

I heard Scottie's voice among it all saying 'Christ'. That was all he said and I hoped he was satisfied. We must get back to base. We hadn't a lot of fuel left and there might be bad weather over base for all we knew. We set course to the north. Scottie came up alongside me on my port side and tucked his wing fairly close in behind me.

We crossed the coastal belt at much the same place as we had come in an hour and a half earlier. In my reflecting mirror on top of the hood I could see the sky still yellow and the light from; the conflagration glowed on the perspex of the hood and showed the arc of the propellor disc. I wasn't going to forget it very easily.

We landed and taxied back to the dispersal area. The mechanics were waiting for us and asked what the score was. I mumbled something quite incoherent and went quickly to the dispersal hut. 'Bish', the IO, was there to greet us and to take down our report. Bish had obviously only just been woken up from what must have been a deep slumber, for he was still only half awake. His hair stood up from the back of his head and his opened shirt and collar, loosened tie, and generally crumpled uniform hardly gave an aura of authority as he began to cross-examine us on our sortie.

The rot set in for me one day in the late summer of 1942, just a week after Scottie had got himself married to a young English girl he had been running around with for some time.

'Who wants to do the dawn patrol?' Spud had asked the previous evening and Scottie had replied, 'I will. We'll get off early.' He had then turned to me and continued, 'Joyce wants you to come out and have a drink with us down at the 'British Lion'. Come on, now. It's gone opening time.'

Had it been any other time I would have agreed willingly, since there was nothing I liked better than drinking with him in the company of his young wife. But as it was I had a splitting headache and particularly wanted to get a good night's sleep. So I said, 'Sorry, Scottie, but any other day.' I said goodnight to him. 'See you tomorrow night anyway at the 'British Lion', were his last words to me before he went to catch the bus. I waved to him as the bus disappeared into the gathering dusk. Even then I felt I had made a mistake. I had a late supper and turned in afterwards.

When I came down to breakfast the following morning it was too late. It had happened. Scottie was dead. He had been shot down by a 109 a few hours earlier on the dawn patrol. There was no doubt of his death. His number two saw him go straight into the sea from only a thousand feet. They were flying about three miles off shore, he told me, and going towards Rye from Dungeness when it happened.

Scottie was on the outside of the two and they were in loose line abreast. This was our customary formation when working in pairs, the idea being that both could observe the other's tail. Number two said that they were flying just beneath cloud base, which was nearly ten tenths. The first intimation he had that all was not well was when he saw two 109s emerge from the cloud and just sit on Scottie's tail. He said he didn't have time to warn Scottie on the R/T about them. 'It all happened so quickly. It was over before I could turn towards them,' he told us, overcome by emotion. 'They went back into the cloud almost before Scottie had hit the water and then I came back to base.'

I was desolate. This was the beginning of the end for me and I knew it. I did my best with Joyce but I couldn't convince her that it was just one of those things and, for that matter, I couldn't convince myself either. I never wanted to see Joyce again.

10

The End of My Flying Days

17 September 1942 was the day when I made my last operational flight. I had passed the point of no return. I was no longer consciously tired. I was an inanimate being actuated only by automatic reflexes. I kept very much to myself and the death wish began to dominate my mind. I was a totally irresponsible agent but I seemed to have acquired a sort of second wind. An unnatural abundance of energy flowed through me and I knew that, if once I let go, I should flounder totally and never recover again, so great would be the reaction. We had only four pilots in the Flight now and we had to be at readiness in our cockpits because the German 'recce' planes and low level fighter-bombers were coming in low over the sea, undetected by radar and inflicting damage on the coastal districts.

Pilots in pairs spent an hour at a time at cockpit readiness and then they were relieved by the other two. We tried to read a magazine or a book or the paper at these times, though it wasn't easy. Tension was about you all the time especially when the hands of your watch crept towards the hour when you were due to be relieved. At about five minutes to the hour the two reliefs would come out of the hut, carrying their helmets and taking the last few puffs of their cigarettes, and you wondered whether they would reach their machines before the alarm bell sounded for take-off. If they did not, you knew damned well that you would have to go yourself.

The MO was not slow to see that I was cracking up, and it wasn't long before I found myself in the RAF hospital at Halton and once again in front of the psychiatrists. Ostensibly I was sent to the hospital because I couldn't sleep, but it became obvious that the doctors were going to detain me for a lengthy period in order to delve more deeply into the reasons for my insomnia and I soon became the plaything of the 'trick cyclists'.

At first I was placed in an ordinary ward with those recovering from illnesses requiring surgery, but before long I was removed to a private room where there was not so much to disturb me.

The first time I was brought before the RAF psychiatrist he seemed genial enough, and very different from the sort of person one would expect a man of his calling to be.

'Well,' he said. 'What's the trouble?'

Such a question, put so casually and tritely, I thought was amusing and I felt tempted to be facetious, but in point of fact I answered in a meek and unconvincing manner, 'I don't know,' like a schoolboy trying to find an answer to a problem set by his master.

I tried to envisage the future, but could see none save that which existed at the lunatic asylums at Netley and Beckenham. It was obvious that I couldn't go back to the outside world in this condition and, if this were so, I must stay in the hospital until I could. The lunatic asylum was therefore a natural sequence to this existence. It was going to be on my own account that I would return to it.

The next day I visited the psychiatrist again and he greeted me in much the same manner as he had done the day before.

'Have you ever had a breakdown before?' he asked me, all of a sudden.

'Yes,' I replied, feeling no longer in any doubt that he had read right through my dossier and had found references there to my sojourns in Netley and Beckenham hospitals. Accordingly, I went on to enlarge upon my experiences there. He was silent whilst I unfolded my tale and, when I had finished, he surprised and dismayed me by informing me that he had not known about this after all. He was silent for a long time after this and remained eyeing me with a quizzical interest.

I later went to Oxford for a week for electro-encephalograms and I was then sent to the Central Medical Board in London for examination.

I had to undergo the full examination – physical as well as mental – which took the whole day, and at the end of this I was brought before a high ranking RAF medical officer. He inspected me gravely and informed me that my flying days were over. This news was hardly unexpected in view of the knowledge he must have acquired of my medical history, and I was only too fully conscious of the manner in which he had acquired it. Once more I was shaken by the consequences of divulging my previous history to the psychiatrist at Halton, but I had still a vain hope that I might reverse the verdict by pleading with him. This I did, lucidly and with great sincerity, but he was quite adamant in his decision. As I looked deeply into his eyes, I saw there, as in a crystal ball, the end of my career and, possibly, of my sanity.

11

Clouds of Fear

My wheel had turned full circle and before long I returned to a Service Psychiatric Hospital at Dumfries in Scotland. The years that intervened since I had left a similar establishment before the war had been full of varying experiences fraught, for the most part with enormous pressures which had condensed a lifetime into a few years. There existed no counterpart to our mode of life in any other sphere of human experience on earth and none could gauge or even hope to intrude into our thoughts who had not lived similarly. Our mental wavelength was unique.

All conspired eventually to produce a loss of faith.

Life and death were no longer the sacred things that once they were to me; perhaps nothing better illustrates this attitude than the episode of Demo's funeral in the summer of 1942.

Demo had been killed when he hit his head on his aircraft's tail-plane as he baled out over Rye Harbour, after the engine of his machine stopped. He died a few minutes after he was picked up by the rescue boat.

Upon General De Gaulle's orders presumably, the Free-French were to give Demo a full ceremonial funeral. Consequently, on the day, six of their top-brass descended upon Hawkinge. They all made for the bar, followed by us. They ranged from General to heaven knows what else in rank but it was painfully obvious to us that they were Office Wallahs with no knowledge of flying.

We were drunk before lunch and scarcely sober afterwards. The ceremony was conducted in the cemetery which lay alongside the aerodrome. The afternoon was lovely, the flowers and trees all at their summer best, with scarcely a cloud in the sky and little noise of any sort apart from human chatter.

I wondered what would happen if the Jerries came over and strafed us. The Station Padre arrived, the Free-French top brass arrived, the firing party arrived, and finally us. The firing party were the only ones who were sober. The last rites were mumbled, the coffin, draped in the Tricolour, was lowered and the firing party fired, the crackle of the blanks alone disturbing the summer air. We all looked grave but I wondered what Demo was thinking for we all had difficulty in standing up. Demo must have laughed; you could never put anything over on Demo.

The ceremony was over; we dispersed to the mess and back to the bar where we resumed our carousal from where it had been so rudely interrupted. No mention was made of Demo as far as I can recall. What a charade it had been. We all got drunk.

Demo wouldn't have wanted all this; none of the others got it, they went quietly into the sea or into some foreign field without fuss or ceremony. This was laid on for political reasons and poor modest Demo had become its unwitting victim; thus was life exploited even in death.

Death was a constant companion; paradoxically because of it life became much sweeter and one felt totally alive, with every faculty exercised and stretched to its fullest extent. Friends died, always the best, yet it didn't seem that they had gone far. They still sat alongside you when you flew and you could sense their presence, their laughter and their vitality, the things they used to say. The temptation to bridge the gap and join them by suicide could easily be disguised; the idea did not seem abhorrent.

There were many others in the hospital from all the three services and all suffered different experiences which produced much the same effect. It took many years to recover completely and it was often a long and painful process.

Despite the physical treatments and the utter devotion of the doctors and nurses there remained one ingredient without which there existed little hope of recovery and that was the love of God, whether by direct communication or through the medium of another. It was available to all; some rejected it, some did not recognise it.

The abiding truth is: 'The eternal God is thy refuge, and underneath are the everlasting arms.'

Sometimes this was obscured by 'Clouds of Fear'.

If I had learnt little else from the past I had learnt that.

I was lucky.

List of Illustrations

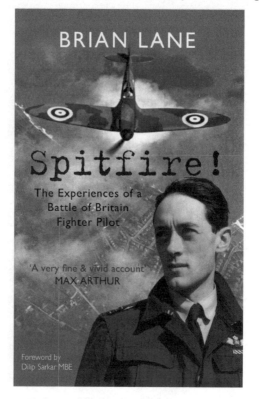

Also available from Amberley Publishing

How to fly the legendary fighter plane in combat using the manuals and instructions supplied by the RAF during the Second World War

Also available from Amberley Publishing

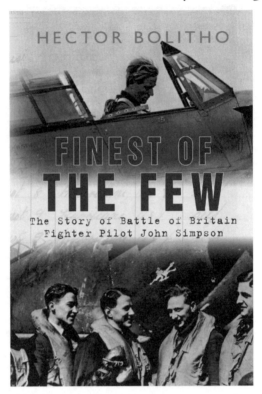

*The remarkable Battle of Britain experiences of fighter pilot
John Simpson, DFC*

Also available from Amberley Publishing

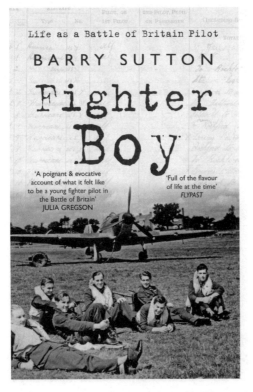

The Battle of Britain memoir of Hurricane pilot Barry Sutton, DFC

'A refreshing book written just after the events' *INTERCOM: THE AIRCREW ASSOCIATION*

'The reader will find in Squadron Leader Sutton the virtues which the country has come to admire in the RAF flier – courage, determination, persistence, unfailing good humour, optimism, faith' *THE TIMES*

At 23 years of age, Barry Sutton had experienced more than the average person experiences in a lifetime. This book, based on a diary he kept during the war, covers September 1939 to September 1940 when he was shot down and badly burned.

£10.99 Paperback
61 illustrations
192 pages
978-1-4456-0627-9

Also available as an ebook
Available from all good bookshops or to order direct
Please call **01453-847-800**
www.amberleybooks.com

Also available from Amberley Publishing

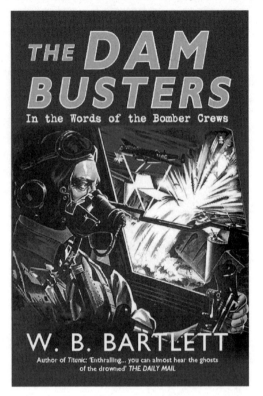

The story of the legendary bouncing-bomb attack on Germany's dams

The Dam Busters raids have gone down as perhaps the most famous air-strikes in history. Yet behind the story of courage and determination there lies another, darker side, both for the aircrews – 40% of whom died in the mission – and for those who lived below the dams in the path of the flood, many of whom were not even German. This new account tells the story of those dramatic events through the eyes of those who were there.

£9.99 Paperback
66 illustrations (32 col)
336 pages
978-1-4456-1193-8

Also available as an ebook
Available from all good bookshops or to order direct
Please call **01453-847-800**
www.amberleybooks.com

Also available from Amberley Publishing

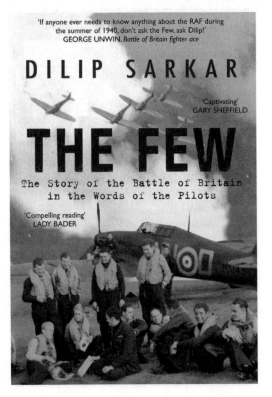

'If anyone ever needs to know anything about the RAF during the summer of 1940, don't ask the Few, ask Dilip!'
GEORGE UNWIN, *Battle of Britain fighter ace*

DILIP SARKAR

'Captivating'
GARY SHEFFIELD

THE FEW

The Story of the Battle of Britain
in the Words of the Pilots

'Compelling reading'
LADY BADER

The history of the Battle of Britain in the words of the pilots

'Over the last 30 years Dilip Sarkar has sought out and interviewed or corresponded with numerous survivors worldwide. Many of these were not famous combatants, but those who formed the unsung backbone of Fighter Command in 1940. Without Dilip's patient recording and collation of their memories, these survivors would not have left behind a permanent record.' LADY BADER

'A well-researched detailed chronicle of the Battle of Britain'. HUGH SEBAG MONTEFIORE

£9.99 Paperback
129 photographs
320 pages
978-1-4456-0701-6

Also available as an ebook

Available from all good bookshops or to order direct
Please call **01453-847-800**
www.amberleybooks.com

Also available from Amberley Publishing

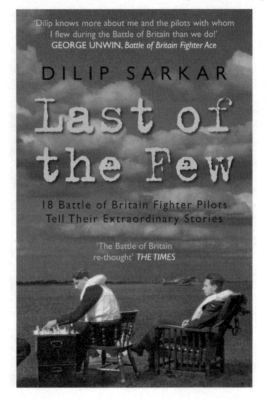

'Dilip knows more about me and the pilots with whom I flew during the Battle of Britain than we do!'
GEORGE UNWIN, *Battle of Britain Fighter Ace*

DILIP SARKAR

Last of the Few

18 Battle of Britain Fighter Pilots Tell Their Extraordinary Stories

'The Battle of Britain re-thought' *THE TIMES*

18 Spitfire and Hurricane fighter pilots recount their experiences of combat during the Battle of Britain

'Dilip knows more about me and the pilots with whom I flew during the Battle of Britain than we do! If anyone ever needs to know anything about the RAF during the summer of 1940, don't ask the Few, ask him!' GEORGE 'GRUMPY' UNWIN, Battle of Britain fighter ace

£9.99 Paperback
55 Photographs
224 pages
978-1-4456-0282-0

Also available as an ebook
Available from all good bookshops or to order direct
Please call **01453-847-800**
www.amberleybooks.com

Also available from Amberley Publishing

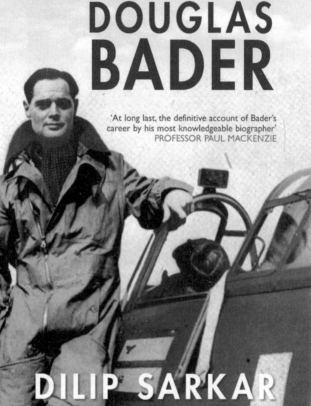

The RAF Fighter Pilot Who Shot Down 20 Enemy
Aircraft Despite Having Lost Both His Legs

DOUGLAS
BADER

'At long last, the definitive account of Bader's
career by his most knowledgeable biographer'
PROFESSOR PAUL MACKENZIE

DILIP SARKAR

Also available from Amberley Publishing

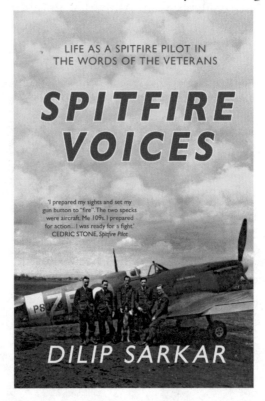

Spitfire fighter pilots tell their extraordinary stories of combat during the Second World War

'I prepared my sights and set my gun button to "fire". The two specks were aircraft. Me 109s. I prepared for action… I was ready for a fight.' CEDRIC STONE, Spitfire Pilot

'There is nothing glamorous in being a fighter pilot. There is nothing glamorous in killing and being killed. Exciting, very exciting, sometimes too exciting, but definitely not glamorous, not even in a Spitfire.' MAURICE MACEY, Spitfire Pilot

£12.99 Paperback
169 Photographs
320 pages
978-1-4456-0695-8

Also available as an ebook
Available from all good bookshops or to order direct
Please call **01453-847-800**
www.amberleybooks.com